Scout Games

Copyright 1999
The Scout Association
Baden-Powell House
Queen's Gate
London SW7 5JS

ISBN 0 85165 309 X

Compiled by David Garton
Edited by Stephen Nixey
Illustrated by Bob Dewar, Rich,
Cover design by Deborah Thomson, Liz Pipe

This edition, first impression 1999

Printed in Great Britain by Thanet Press Limited

CONTENTS

Foreward...............................	4
Introduction	5
Everybody In!........................	7
Knockout Games	11
Pairs Games...........................	18
Two-team Games....................	31
Patrol Competitions	40
Interactive Games...................	45
Races	47
Relays	52
Sports Games	64
Run Scoring Games	74
Scoring Rounders	79
Wide Games...........................	84
Raids	105
Training Games......................	111
Games Key	117
Index	118

FOREWARD

This book is based on the hugely popular title *Scout Games* which was first published in 1972 by The Scout Association. Over the years, many games within that book have been developed and adapted and some have for various reasons, become outdated.

The games in this book represent the very best of the original selection plus some new variations and all have been tried and tested, and altered if necessary. There are dozens of additional games which have all proved popular with Scouts and which deserve a place in this book. Many thanks to the contributors of SCOUTING Magazine for their suggestions for games to include. Our apologies to anyone who claims to have invented a game in this book, or included it in another collection of games - collecting games is a bit like Chinese whispers and one is never sure enough of a source to be able to credit it!

Whilst the terms used in this book refer specifically to the Scout Section, most games can be used with little, if any, alteration to suit the other age ranges within the Scout Group.

If you have any favourite games which are not included in this book but which may be considered for inclusion in a future edition, please send your ideas to: Scout Games, The Publications Department, The Scout Association, Baden-Powell House, Queen's Gate, London SW7 5JS.

David Garton
1999

INTRODUCTION

Games are an important part of Troop meetings and they often require planning and preparation to ensure they work well. Advice is given at the start of each of the specific games sections, but here are a few tips to consider beforehand.

- **Choosing a game**

Games can be used for many purposes - encouraging team work, building the Patrol spirit, reinforcing training skills or to teach a new skill in a *fun* way. A fast, active game allows the Troop to 'let off steam', while a quieter game can be used to calm an 'active' Troop down. You need to select games carefully reflecting the mix and ability of the Troop to achieve the results required. Where possible avoid asking the Troop 'what game would you like to play now?' as the usual answer of 'football' will only disappoint Members when they play something different.

- **Be ready to start on time**

Make sure you have the required equipment checked and ready in plenty of time beforehand. Equally important, ensure that the person running the game knows what they have to do in good time.

- **Explaining how to play the game**

At the beginning of a meeting, get everyone's attention and explain all the rules of the game to them. Make sure all the rules understood by the participants and that the players fully appreciate the limits within which the game should be played and indeed why there are limits.

- **Running the game**

In any game that requires an adjudicator, Scouts will expect the expertise of a 'world class' referee or umpire.

Winning is important so if you are running the game watch it closely. Decide in advance how you will remember who has and has not had a 'go' and what action to take if someone cheats or there is a foul.

• How long should the game run?

The general rule of thumb is that you should end a game while it is still being enjoyed. It is however important to make sure that everybody has been involved and had a 'turn'. Remember, run a game for too long and the Scouts will start losing interest.

• Winners and losers

While there are many cooperative games where no-one has to be a loser, many people enjoy the competitive element of a team game or individual challenge. Decide how you are going to 'reward' the winners - and the losers, for sometimes it is worthwhile allocating points for participating well rather than just winning. Where the game is structured like a knockout competition it is advisable to organise another activity or game for those members who have been 'knocked out' so they have another chance to compete. Likewise it is important to avoid having the situation of where the same Scout always seems to lose.

• Safety first

Always look carefully at the environment in which you are going to 'play' in and undertake a risk assessment. If you have any concerns always consult **Policy, Organisation and Rules**. It is certainly worth considering: whether the hall is large enough? could a player collide with with fixed furniture? is the ball soft enough? is the floor too slippery? could glass get broken and so on. And as stated on the *Young People First* 'Code of Behaviour' yellow card, you should not play physical games with young people in your charge.

• How well did it go?

Take a few minutes to note down after the event how well the game went. Ask yourself if the game could have been run differently and if the Scouts enjoyed and why?

If the Leader concerned applies these principles it should be possible to provide challenging, adventurous games that are attractive to Members which at the same time don't generate accident reports.

EVERYBODY IN!

These are games in which the Troop play as individuals against each other.

Trader

Equipment: Coloured counters e.g. tiddly-winks, paper squares.
Players: Any number.

- Each player is issued with four different coloured counters.
- Sets of counters are worth the following points:

10 points - 4 white counters
8 points - 4 yellow counters
6 points - 4 green counters
5 points - 4 red counters
3 points - 3 counters of any colour
1 point - 2 counters of any colour

- The value of black counters is variable and will be announced by the game leader at the end of each trading session.
- Players try to increase the value of their holdings by trading one counter at a time with any other player. Each player hides a counter in one hand and shows it at the same time as the other player.
- Players must exchange counters once they have been revealed. All trades are final!
- Players sit down when they no longer wish to trade.
- The player (or team) with the highest score at the end of each trading session is the winner. The game leader should keep a running total to find the overall winner at the end of the game.

Dodger

Equipment: A ball.
Players: Any number.

• Choose four players who stand with their hands on the waist of the player in front. The last player in the line is known as 'dodger'.
• The other players stand in a circle surrounding the line of four players and attempt to hit dodger below the knee with the ball. Players should quickly pass the ball across the circle to set up another player If they do not have a good opportunity to hit dodger themselves.
• Anyone who hits dodger takes position at the front of the line of four. At the same time dodger must return to the circle.
• The player who was originally third in the line consequently becomes the new dodger.

Off Ground Tag

Equipment: Chairs (three less than the number of players) spaced over the playing area.
Players: Any number.

• Choose a player to be 'it'.
• The aim of the game is to avoid getting tagged by 'it'.
• A chair represents a safe area where players cannot be tagged provided both their feet are off the floor.
• When no spare chairs are available, any player without a chair may become 'safe' by touching a player who is already on a chair. At this point the player on the chair may now be tagged and must find another chair. Once a player steps off a chair, the other player must step on immediately or risk being tagged. Anyone who is tagged must take over as 'it'.

Knock Off Ground Tag

Equipment: Chairs (three less than the number of players) spaced over the playing area.
Players: Any number.

• Play as for the previous game.
• Tagged players sit down on one of the chairs so that they and the chair are out of play.
• The last untagged player wins the game and becomes the new 'it' for the next game.

Pick It Up

Equipment: Any soft object.
Players: 12 upwards.

• Players sit in a circle and number off around it - one, two, three, four... one, two, three, four... in such a way that three or more players have the same corresponding number.
• Players start each game sitting down, with legs crossed.
• The game leader randomly calls out a number.
• Players whose number corresponds to that called out stand up and run clockwise round the outside of the circle.
• On returning to the gap where they were sitting, players enter into the circle and attempt to be the first to pick the object off the ground.
• The player who achieves the most 'pick-ups' (after equal turns) is the winner.

Six

Equipment: A die, a bar of chocolate (unopened) on a plate, a knife, a fork, a pair of gloves and a few other articles of clothing (optional).
Players: Eight or more.

- Players sit in a circle and throw the die in turn, passing it on clockwise.
- Anyone throwing a six goes to the centre, puts on the clothing and tries to cut a piece of chocolate to eat using the knife and fork.
- As soon as another player throws a six, the player in the circle must remove the gloves and extra clothing and return to his or her place in the circle.
- Any players who manage to satisfy their appetites are considered to be the winners!

You can apply the game to any task that can be continued from one player to the next. This could include training activities.

Casualty

Equipment: Bandages, die, a stopwatch.
Players: Any number.

- On throwing a six, players bandage up a patient (a volunteer) sitting in the centre of the circle, e.g. apply head, hand, arm, knee or foot bandages.
- The player who applies the greatest amount of bandage correctly in a given time wins the game.

KNOCKOUT GAMES

These are games in which the objective is for individual players, teams or Patrols to try to knock opponents out of the game in some fashion, whereby the winner is the last remaining player.

Kingball

Equipment: A ball.
Players: Any number.

- Players spread out around the playing area.
- A player is nominated to become 'Kingball' whose role is to hit other players below the knee with the ball.
- The other players try to dodge the ball.
- Players hit by the ball help Kingball to hit the other players.
- The last remaining player is the winner and becomes Kingball for the next game.

Confined Kingball

Equipment: A ball.
Players: Any number.

- Mark out a set area - a square or circle will do.
- The player throwing the ball must stay on the outside, whilst other players are confined to the inside of the area making it more difficult to avoid the ball.
- Players hit by the ball help the original thrower to hit the other players.
- The last remaining player is the winner.

Punchball

Equipment: A ball.
Players: Ten or more.

• Players stand in a circle with their feet at least three ball widths apart and touching those of the players either side of them.
• To start or restart play, the game leader randomly throws the ball into the centre of the circle.
• With one hand only, players try to punch the ball between the legs of another player.
• Players must keep one hand behind their back at all times.
• Players must drop out of the game if the ball passes between their legs.
• The last remaining pair of players are the winners.

Continuous Punchball

Equipment: A ball.
Players: Ten or more.

• Players stand in a circle with their feet at least three ball widths apart and touching those of the players either side of them.
• With one hand only, players try to punch a ball between the legs of the other players.
• Players score one point if they successfully hit the ball between another player's legs.
• If the ball passes between their own legs they lose a point but do not drop out.
• The player who scores the most points in the agreed playing time wins the game.

Backwards Punchball

Equipment: A ball.
Players: Ten or more.

• Play Knockout or Continuous Punchball as above, but stand facing outwards.
• Punch the ball by bending over forwards and knocking it back into the circle.
• Players must drop out of the game if the ball passes between their legs.
• The last remaining pair of players are the winners.

Crowded Circle

Equipment: Whistle.
Players: Any number.

• Mark out three large circles and number them accordingly.
• Players move at random around the room.
• The game leader turns out the lights and calls out a circle number.
• Players continue to move until they think they are standing inside the circle corresponding to the correct number.
• Anyone with any part of their body outside the circle when the lights are turned back on must drop out of the game.
• Continue with shorter periods of darkness.
• The last remaining player is the winner.
• Alternatively - leave the lights on, but decrease the size of the circles, whereupon the whistle, Scouts have five seconds to get inside the circles.
• As the circles get smaller Scouts will have to co-operate more with each other to maximise the number that can fit into the circle.

Poison

Equipment: Any large, soft object.
Players: Any number.

• Players stand in a circle and link up with the players either side of them by grasping their wrists.
• A large, soft object - the 'poison' is placed in the centre of the circle.
• Players try to pull each other towards the poison.
• Players are out of the game if they touch the poison or break the link between them and their neighbour(s), no matter who broke the link first.
• The last remaining player is the winner.
• Start a new game for Scouts 'out' in a clear part of the area.

Link-ball

Equipment: A ball (or beanbag).
Players: Eight or more.

• Players stand in a circle and link up to the players either side of them by grasping their wrists.
• Players attempt to kick the ball (or beanbag) between the legs of any other player in the circle.
• Players are out of the game if the ball goes between their own legs or if the link between them and their neighbour(s) is broken, no matter who broke the link first.
• The last remaining player is the winner.

Dividing Amoebae

Equipment: None.
Players: Eight or more

- Two players are chosen to be the 'amoeba' and link arms to become a pair.
- The rest of the players spread out around the playing area.
- When the game commences the amoeba attempts to tag the other players, who run around to avoid being tagged.
- Tagged players must link arms with the amoeba thus forming a chain.
- Every time the amoeba becomes four players, it divides into two separate pairs and the new pair(s) join the chase to tag the remaining 'free' players.
- The last untagged player is the winner.

Grab

Equipment: Soft objects, e.g. hanks of rope or beanbags.
Players: Six or more.

- Enough objects for all but one of the players are placed in the centre of the room. (For large groups of players make more than one pile or scatter the objects around the room to avoid collisions between players.)
- Players move clockwise around the room, keeping their left hand in contact with the wall.
- On the command '*Grab*' players must try to retrieve one of the objects.
- Players failing to retrieve an object drop out of the game.
- An object is removed and the game recommences.
- The last remaining player is the winner.

Runaround Quiz

Equipment: A set of questions taken from a quiz book, quiz game or some made up.
Players: Any number.

• This is an energetic version of a simple quiz game run for fun or training purposes.
• Mark out three well spaced circles - A, B and C on the floor or nominate three corners.
• Players start off in the centre of the playing area.
• The game leader poses a question to the whole group and gives three alternative answers - A, B and C.
• Players have just ten seconds to choose the answer which they think is correct and run to the appropriate circle (or corner) that corresponds to the answer.
• When the game leader calls '*Runaround*' players have a further five seconds to change their mind.
• Players with the correct answer return to the centre and wait for the next question. Those who are incorrect must drop out of the game.
• The last remaining player scores two points.
• If all the remaining players are incorrect, they score one point each.
• Restart the game when there is only one or no players left in the round.
• The player who scores the most points at the end of a session is the individual winner. Total up individual points to find the winning Patrol.
• As a tip keep aside some suitably difficult questions to pose if a round is becoming a little too long.

Head It! Catch It!

Equipment: A ball.
Players: Any number.

• Players stand in a circle around the game leader.
• The game leader shouts '*Head it*' or '*Catch it*' prior to throwing the ball to a player.
• The player to whom the ball is thrown must carry out the opposite instruction to that shouted out.
• Players who carry out the instruction called, must sit down.
• The last player standing is the winner.

PAIRS GAMES

These games are for the whole Troop and involve one pair of players competing against each other at a time.

In this type of game it is usual, but not essential, that each player in the competing pair represents a team. This makes the game much more exciting for those spectating. Teams may offer vocal support but otherwise each player competes unaided. These 'duels' are very popular with many Scouts as they are seen as a test of personal skill. To the victor they are a great morale booster but it is important to realise that they can have quite the opposite effect too, especially if a Scout happens to be physically or intellectually disadvantaged.

As far as possible Scouts should be matched by ability. Challenges that involve physical strength are usually best avoided except where success is based on luck or cunning (i.e. out-smarting an opponent). For most competitions it is recommended that both teams order themselves by height for physically based competitions, or age for intellectually based competitions.

Pairs games can be used for training purposes. Not only do Scouts get the chance to try an activity for themselves but they can learn by watching how everybody else does it too!

Note: The first game 'Duel' should be used as a blueprint for all the following games in this section.

Duel

Equipment: Varied.
Players: Twelve or more, although teams should be made up of equal numbers.

• Players divide into two teams and stand facing each other along opposite sides of the playing area.
• Players then number off from the left hand end of each line.
• The game leader calls out a player's number at random.
• The two players with that number go to the centre of the room and compete against each other.
• The winning player scores a point for his or her team.
• The team with the most points overall at the end of the game wins.

Pair's Hockey

Equipment: Two hockey sticks, a ball or puck, two chairs positioned at opposite ends of the room.
Players: Six or more.

• Start the game by following steps one to four from the Duel game outlined above.
• Opponents play hockey against each other using chair legs as goals, shooting towards the goal to their team's right.
• The first to score a goal wins a point for their team.
• The team with the most points after the allotted time is the winner.

Dog And Bone

Equipment: Any small object placed in the centre (a hat or glove is ideal).
Players: Six or more.

• Start the game by following steps one to four from the Duel game outlined above.
• Place the small object in the centre of your playing area.
• Players must try to grab the object and get it safely to a wall to the right of their team without getting tagged by their opponents.
• If players do not have a clear opportunity to grab the object, then they can try to outsmart their opponent's with some dummy manoeuvres.
• Points are awarded for either getting the object to the wall without getting tagged or for tagging an opponent after he/she has touched the object.
• The team with the most points when the game ends is the winner.

Point Of No Return

Equipment: One skittle or similar object per player.
Players: Any number.

• In the play area mark out a single line.
• Keeping their feet firmly behind the marked line, the players must place their skittle as far as possible in front of the line. Pushing or throwing the skittle is not allowed.
• The winner is the person who places the skittle furthest from the line without any part of their body touching the floor beyond the line.

Bull's-eye

Equipment: None.
Players: Six or more.

• Draw four large concentric circles on the floor just like on a target, i.e. 'bull' (five points), 'inner' (four points), 'magpie' (three points), 'outer' (two points).
• Keeping their arms folded at all times, players and opponents must compete to place themselves on the highest scoring position on the target.
• After exactly 30 seconds the game leader calls '*Freeze*'.
• Players are awarded points in accordance with the position of their respective highest scoring foot.
• The team with the most points at the end of the game is the winner.

Robin And Little John

Equipment: A wide rope.
Players: Six or more.

• Divide the players into two teams of equal strength and form team lines.
• Lay the rope down the centre of the floor of the playing area parallel to the team lines. (The game could also be played on a small fallen tree, plank, or a simple chalk line on the floor, etc.)
• Opponents go to the end of the rope to the left of their respective team.
• They then walk along the rope and try to unbalance each other when they meet.
• Any player who makes it from one end of the rope to the other without 'falling off' wins a point for his or her team.
• The team with the most points at the end of the game is the winner.

Barge

Equipment: None.
Players: Any number.

- Divide the players into two teams.
- Players, hopping on one leg with their arms folded, must try to unbalance their opponent in this duel.
- Players may not change their hopping leg.
- Points are awarded to players who force their opponent to unfold his or her arms or to touch the floor with any part of the body other than the hopping foot.
- The team with the most points at the end of the game is the winner.

Matchbox

Equipment: Two empty matchboxes.
Players: Six or more.

- Each player must lay a matchbox horizontally on the back of one hand and keep it balanced there.
- Opponents must then try to knock off the other person's matchbox without dislodging their own.
- Points are awarded for each matchbox knocked off.
- The team with the most points at the end of the game is the winner.

Snatch And Grab

Equipment: None.
Players: Eight or more.

- Divide all the players into two teams.
- Players should face each other, on a soft floor surface, in a 'press-up' position with arms locked straight.
- Players must then try to take away each others' support.
- The first player to cause his or her opponent to fall from the press-up position wins a point.
- The team who scores the most points during the game is the winner.

Stave Tug

Equipment: One stave positioned centrally and parallel to team lines.
Players: Any number.

- Players go to the end of the stave to the left of their team and grab the end of the stave with one hand only.
- They must then try to touch the wall to their team's right, without letting go of the stave.
- The first player to reach his or her team's wall wins. Any player who lets go of the stave automatically loses the game.

Pillow Fight

Equipment: One pillow per player.
Players: Six or more.

• In the designated play area mark out a circle for each player one pace across and two paces apart (or stand players on small crates, or similar).
• Players must try to unbalance each other using the pillow as a weapon.
• The winner is the first person to force his or her opponent out of their circle.

Poke And Push

Equipment: Two staves and one beanbag.
Players: Six or more.

• Divide the players into teams and place the staves and beanbag in the centre of the playing area.
• Each player from each team must try to gain possession of the beanbag using only their staves.
• The first person to push the beanbag all the way to the wall to the right of their team wins a point.

Ankle Push

Equipment: None.
Players: Six or more.

• Mark out a circle approximately four paces across.
• Players must grab their own ankles with their hands and lean against their opponent.
• The first player to force an opponent to step out of the circle or to let go of their ankles wins a point for their team.

Training Miscellany

Equipment: Varied.
Players: Six or more, depending on the type of challenge.

• Get all the players to undertake a given challenge (see examples below).
• Or, different pairs could undertake different challenges.
• To speed up the game, more than one pair could be called out at a time to undertake the challenge.
• The first player to complete the activity wins a point for their team.
• The team with the most points is the winner.

Challenges - you could choose from:
• Tie a bowline.
• Break a given code.
• Write down four of the Scout Laws.
• Identify a constellation.
• Name the feature at a given grid reference.
• Correctly set a map.
• Take the bearing of a given object.
• Roll up a flag for breaking.
• Pack away a Trangier.
• Put a person into the recovery position.
• Make a sling from your neckerchief.
• Make a pressure pad from a strip of cloth.
• Coil and throw a rope to hit a given target.
• Fold up a tent into it's bag.
• Lace up a pair of walking boots.

Jockey

Equipment: None.
Players: Eight or more.

• Players find a partner of similar stature and number themselves off as number one and number two.
• A circle is then formed with number ones standing in front of the number twos.
• The game leader calls out a number and those with that number move clockwise in a circle.
• The game leader then calls out '*Jockeys mount*' and players continue to move clockwise until they reach their partners, at which point they mount their partner piggy-back style.
• The last pair to mount successfully drop out.
• The last pair remaining in the game are the winners.

Hare And Hound

Equipment: None.
Players: Ten or more.

• Players stand in a circle except for one player who is chosen to be the 'hare'.
• The hare walks clockwise around the outside of the circle and taps the shoulder of any player, who then becomes the 'hound'.
• The hare must then run around the circle and back to the space vacated by the hound.
• The hound must try to catch the hare before he or she makes it around the circle.
• If the hare makes it without getting caught, then the game continues. If the hare is caught by the hound, the hound then become the new hare.
• The most successful hare is the winner.

Cambridge Boat Race

Equipment: None.
Players: Ten or more.

• Players sit in two lines, with shoes off, in such a way that each player is facing another player with their feet touching.
• Players facing each other are numbered off as pairs down the lines.
• The game leader calls out a number and players with that number stand up, run around the outside of their lines - the 'boat' and back up the centre stepping over players' legs until they return to their place.
• The first player back, in each round, is the winner.

In And Out Of The Houses

Equipment: None.
Players: Eight or more.

• Nominate a player to be the 'escapee' and another to be the 'pursuer'.
• The other players pair off and scatter about the playing area, with one partner standing immediately in front of the other.
• On the command 'Go,' the pursuer chases the escapee.
• If the pursuer tags the escapee, their roles are immediately reversed.
• To avoid being tagged, the escapee may stand in front of another pair of players. The player at the back of the pair then becomes the escapee.
• Tip - for larger numbers of players run the game with two pursuers and two escapees.

Tip And Run

Equipment: None.
Players: Six or more.

• Players divide into two teams and sit in two rows facing each other across an imaginary halfway line.
• The game leader nominates a player, who stands up and touches the shoulder of any member of the opposite team.
• Both players then run to touch both end walls, in either order, and return to their place in the line.
• The first player back scores a point.
• The second player touches the shoulder of an opposing player and so on.
• The team that gains the most points in the time allowed wins.

Pair's Long Goal

Equipment: A football.
Players: 12 or more.

• Mark a goal line behind each team (or use the end walls if playing indoors).
• Divide the players into two teams who stand in two lines across the centre of the room facing each other. Teams should be approximately five to ten paces apart.
• Number off down the team lines from the left.
• The game leader calls out a number.
• Players with the corresponding number go into the centre area and play handball against each other.
• The remaining players must link arms and defend the 'goal' behind them by moving from side to side to block shots.
• Once a goal has been scored a new pair is chosen.
• The team with the most goals in the time allowed wins.

Pair Swap

Equipment: A chair for each player except one.
Players: Eight or more.

• Players sit in a circle, either on the floor or on chairs and are numbered off into two halves so that there are two players for each number sitting approximately opposite each other.
• A chosen player sits in the centre of the circle.
• The game leader calls a number and the players with that number try to change places with each other before the centre player can take one of their places.
• The person who fails to get a place must sit in the centre and try to regain a place at the next call.

Quiz Swap

Equipment: None.
Players: Any number.

• Players sit in a circle, either on the floor or on chairs and are numbered off into two teams.
• Play the game as above, but each player is given a different name based on a theme, e.g. colours, countries or letters.
• The game leader asks a question, the answer to which, will define a pair of players (e.g. 'Which colours appear on the flag of Switzerland?'; 'Which two countries are part of the Commonwealth?'; 'Which two letters appear twice in the Address?').
• The appropriate players try to change places before the player in the centre tries to fill the vacated place.

Tom And Jerry (Cat And Mouse)

Equipment: A watch with a second hand.
Players: Twelve or more.

• The game leader nominates two players as Tom and Jerry.
• The other players stand in a grid formation (rows and columns) approximately one-and-a-half arms lengths away from those to the front, back and sides of them.
• Everybody faces the same direction and grasps the arms of the players either side of them to form 'corridors'.
• Tom must attempt to catch Jerry, who runs up and down the corridors to avoid being caught.
• At 15 second intervals, the game leader calls '*Change*,' whereby those forming the corridors take a quarter turn clockwise linking arms with players now to their left and right .
• Tom must attempt to catch Jerry in under 90 seconds. Tom is replaced after the 90 seconds or once the mouse has been caught. Jerry always stays on until caught.
• Any Tom who catches Jerry and any Jerry who outwits Tom is a winner.

TWO-TEAM GAMES

Games in which the Troop divides into two competing teams. For more examples of two-team games see Sports Games.

Zone Ball

Equipment: A football.
Players: Eight or more.

• Mark out the playing area into four parallel zones of equal size - A, B, C and D.
• Divide the players into two teams - team one and team two.
• Team one stand in zone B; team two stand in zone C.
• The teams try to get the opposing team out by throwing the football and hitting them below the knee.
• If a player's throw is caught, that player must go to zone D (if a member of team one) or zone A (if a member of team two).
• Players in the outer zones can still take an active part in the game and dismiss their opponents with the ball.
• Players must not pick up the ball if it is outside their zone.
• The first team to dismiss all members of the opposing team from the centre zone (B or C) is the winner.

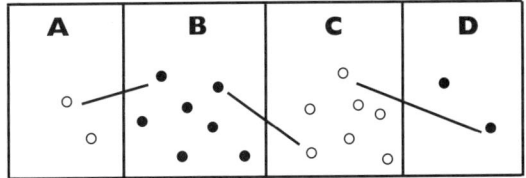

Thrower-catcher

Equipment: Four to six tennis balls.
Players: Eight or more.

• Mark out a centre line.
• Players are divided into two teams the 'throwers' and 'catchers' - and stand in opposite halves of the playing area.
• Throwers form a queue and take turns throwing the ball into the opposition's half, aiming to strike catchers below the knee.
• Catchers who are struck below the knee must drop out of the game.
• If a catcher catches the ball the thrower must drop out of the game.
• The winner is the first team to dismiss all the players from the opposing team.

Run The Risk

Equipment: Enough balls for half of total number of players.
Players: Eight or more.

• Players divide into two teams - dodgers and throwers.
• Each thrower is given a ball and stands with one foot against either of the end walls.
• Dodgers stand with one foot against one of the side walls.
• When the game leader shouts the command '*Fire*,' dodgers run to the opposite wall while throwers try to hit them below the knee with their balls.
• Any dodgers hit below the knee must drop out of the game.
• Any dodgers touching the wall are 'safe.'
• Throwers are given a few seconds in which to attempt to recover their balls before the command to fire is repeated.
• Throwers only fire when they have a foot against the wall.

- Any throwers who are slow in retrieving a ball and get hit by their team's fire must drop out of the game.
- The command '*Fire*' is repeated and the dodgers must again run to the opposite wall avoiding being hit beneath the knee by a ball.
- Each time the dodgers make a successful run they score a point.
- When all of the dodgers are out, the teams swap over.
- The team that scores the most points is the winner.

Human Noughts And Crosses

Equipment: Nine chairs.
Players: Six or more.

- Set the chairs up in a square 3 x 3 formation.
- Divide the players into two teams - 'noughts' and 'crosses'.
- Noughts and crosses take turns to go to the grid and choose a chair to sit on.
- The teams compete in trying to complete a line of three noughts or crosses either horizontally, vertically or diagonally.
- The game should be played in total silence! Players must remember if seated players are noughts or crosses.
- At the end of each game seated players must return, in order, to the back of their respective queues.
- Start each new game with the next player from the defeated team.
- The team recording the most wins in the agreed playing time is the winner.

Submarines

Equipment: Blindfolds.
Players: Eight or more.

- Players divide into two teams - 'submarines' and 'harbour guards'.
- Guards stand blindfolded in a row across the width of the room with their legs wide apart and their feet touching those of the guards next to them guarding the 'harbour'.
- Submarines must endeavour to enter the harbour, i.e. by passing between the legs of the harbour guards.
- Any harbour guard who detects a submarine passing below must bend down and touch it.
- If a harbour guard guesses incorrectly, he or she must drop out of the game.
- If a submarine is detected, it must drop out of the game.
- Submarines must pass in and out of the harbour as many times as possible without being detected.
- Teams swap over once all members of either team are out of the game.
- The team that achieves the most successful passages in and out of the harbour wins the game.

Guardian of the Jewel

Equipment: Blindfolds, objects to represent jewels.
Players: Eight or more.

- Thieves attempt to steal as many jewels as possible from blind guardians (blindfolded and sitting cross legged with jewels placed directly in front).
- Guardians may continually point at where they think the thieves are around them but must remain cross-legged.
- Any jewel thief who is pointed at must drop out.
- The most successful thief and guardian win the game.

Lead Football

Equipment: An unbreakable object weighing about one - two kgs, such as a sandbag or weighted ball.
Players: Six or more.

- Mark out a centre-line on the ground.
- Players are divided into two teams and form team queues outside the playing area.
- Start with the object on the halfway line.
- Alternating between teams, players come forward and stand on the spot where they find the object resting. Balancing the object on their foot, they must kick or flick the object as far as possible into the opponent's half.
- The team that has the object lying in their half after each player has had a turn loses the game.

Defend the Garrison

Equipment: One ball.
Players: Eight or more.

- Divide players into two teams - 'attackers' and 'defenders' and mark out a large circle on the ground the 'garrison'.
- The defenders positioned inside the garrison try to defend it for as long as possible against the attackers.
- Attackers positioned outside the circle throw the ball and aim to hit a defenders leg below the knee. Attackers not in a good position, may throw the ball to better positioned attackers, but they are not allowed inside the garrison.
- Defenders may defend with their hands but, if hit below the knee, or step outside the garrison, they are out of the game.
- When no player is left to defend the garrison, attackers and defenders swap over roles.
- The team that defends the garrison for the longest set period is the winner.

Cowboys And Indians

Equipment: None.
Players: Eight or more.

• Define a safe area at either end of the playing area. You could use a wall or mark out an area.
• Players divide into two teams - 'cowboys' and 'Indians'.
• The two teams standing in rows, face each other across an imaginary halfway line.
• The game leader will instruct you to move backwards or forwards. For example, *'Indians two paces back, cowboys three paces forwards, Indians two paces forwards.'*
• When the game leader eventually instructs *'Cowboys advance'* or *'Indians retreat'* for example, these are signals for cowboys to chase Indians to the Indian safe area.
• If a chaser tags a player before they reach their safe area, they drop out of the game.
• The team that dismisses all members of the opposite side is the winner.
• For a variation anyone who is tagged transfers to the other team and continues playing.
• The side which has most players at the end of the game is the winner.

The Great Divide

Equipment: A coin.
Players: Six or more.

• Widthwise across the centre of the playing area chalk out two parallel lines, two paces apart. The area between the two lines is the 'Great Divide'.
• Define a safe area approximately 15 paces behind each line. You could use a wall or mark out an area.
• Divide players into two teams - 'eastsiders' and 'westsiders' - which stand opposite sides of the divide in rows, with one of their feet just touching the boundary line in front.
• The game leader will toss a coin, allowing it to drop into the divide. Everyone must watch carefully to see how it lands.
• If the coin lands heads up, westsiders cross the divide and chase eastsiders. If it lands tails up, eastsiders cross the divide and chase westsiders.
• Chasers must try to tag one or more players from the other team before they reach their safe area.
• If a player is tagged before reaching their safe area they drop out of the game.
• The side that dismisses all members of the opposite team is the winner.
• For a variation anyone who is tagged transfers to the other team and continues playing.
• The side which has most players at the end of the game is the winner.

Ring Of Steel

Equipment: A ball.
Players: Eight or more.

• Divide the players into two teams, A and B. Remember to swap over the teams roles after an agreed period of time.
• Mark out a circle on the ground that is large enough so that when team A stands on the circle there is space for plenty of gaps. Team B occupies the area outside team A's circle, except for one member, who must position themselves inside it.
• The player from team B in the centre of the circle must try to pass the ball to another member of their team outside it and back again. The pass will only count if it is below shoulder height. Points are awarded for a successfully returned pass.
• Team A must try to intercept the passes. If they successfully stop a pass, they must throw the ball back immediately to the player in the centre.
• The team that scores the most points in the period of time allocated is declared the winner.

Overtake

Equipment: Two balls.
Players: Eight or more.

• Form a standing circle and create two teams by numbering off one, two, one, two, etc.
• The game leader gives one ball to a player in team 'one' and the other ball to a player on team 'two' who are positioned on the opposite side of the circle.
• On the signal '*Start*' teams pass the ball as fast as they can in a clockwise direction around their team (i.e. to alternate players in the circle).
• The team that can get its ball past the other team first, wins.

Game For A Laugh

Equipment: A coin.
Players: Six or more.

- Divide the players into two teams - 'heads' and 'tails'.
- Get the two teams to stand in two parallel lines, two paces apart, widthwise across the centre of the designated playing area.
- The game leader then tosses a coin. If it lands heads up, the 'heads' team must laugh and smile whilst 'tails' must remain solemn (and vice versa).
- Any player on the solemn side who laughs must transfer to the other team.
- After 20 seconds or so repeat this by tossing the coin again.
- The side with the most players at the end of the game is declared the winner.

PATROL COMPETITIONS

These are games in which three or more small teams compete together. Many of the games from the previous section can be played between Patrols on a league or heat basis. The main attribute of the games in this section is that all Patrols in your Troop can compete against each other at the same time. Patrol Games that require a larger area than a simple field are covered in the section on wide games.

Inter-Patrol Games - some ideals!
As Patrols are usually equally matched in terms of age and experience, the Patrol unit is a great asset to game play. Conversely it might be said that games are a great asset to the Patrol! Games can help a Patrol develop by encouraging it's members to interact, to support one another, to tolerate others' weaknesses and appreciate their strengths. For the Patrol Leader, games are an opportunity to practice leadership skills - developing a 'game plan', encouraging, coaching, humouring and captaining their team.

Of course in the real world we can all fall short of the ideals of fair play, good sportsmanship and tolerance. Even so, these must be worked towards - they are far more important goals than those scored in a game! Instances of cheating, arguing with decisions, intolerance towards other players and being a bad loser should not be accepted as part of the norm!

Interactive Complete Patrol Games
In the following games the whole Patrol work together in competing against other Patrols.

Storm The Castle

Equipment: None.
Players: As Patrols - or players divided into three teams.

• Get all the players to link hands to form a circle - the 'castle' and leave one Patrol remaining outside.
• The Patrol outside aims to storm the castle by attempting to get its Patrol members inside the circle as quickly as possible.
• Repeat the activity allowing each Patrol in turn to have the opportunity to storm the castle.
• The Patrol that records the quickest time for storming the castle is the winner.

Balloon Blow

Equipment: One balloon per Patrol.
Players: As Patrols.

• Patrols inflate their balloons and throw them into the air.
• Without touching the balloon, teams prevent it from touching the floor, another player or any other object, by standing beneath it and blowing to keep it airborne.
• The Patrol who manages to keep its balloon in the air for the longest period of time wins.

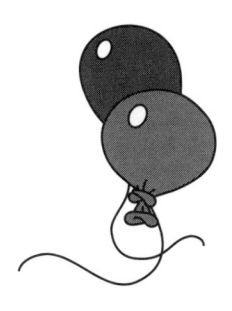

Multi-team Tug Of War

Equipment: Rope, any small object per Patrol.
Player: As Patrols - or players divided into three teams.

• First, securely tie the ends of the rope together, forming a circle.
• Assign an equal portion of the rope circle to each Patrol or team involved.
• Position a small object about four or five paces behind each Patrol's section of rope.
• Each Patrol 'takes the strain' by taking up its section of the rope.
• On the signal '*start*' players try pulling towards their object, preventing the other Patrols from moving towards theirs.
• The first Patrol to lift up their object whilst holding onto the rope wins.

Trading Post

Equipment: Paper money or tokens, simple materials that can be practically turned into useful items, e.g. rope to construct a bowline; water, tea-bag, milk, cup, heater - to make a warm drink; staves and sisal - to construct a tripod; paper and pens - to write ten programme ideas for Troop nights; paper - to make a water container.
Players: Eight or more.

• Get Patrols to produce two lists - a price list of raw materials purchasable from the trading post. Prices should be based on quantities where appropriate e.g. a price per metre of rope. And a list of end products that will be purchased by the trading post with the maximum purchase price that will be offered. *Note:* The price should be more than the total cost of

the raw materials and appropriate to the effort applied in producing the finished item.
- The Leader or older Scouts act as the trading post personnel, setting up the trading post with a well stocked store of raw materials, and provides each Patrol with an appropriate amount of spending money - a 'financial loan'.
- Each Patrol is provided with a copy of the two lists - 'raw materials' and 'finished end products' and then purchases items as required from the trading post.
- Any items made by Patrols for 'resale' to the trading post should be inspected for quality control, e.g. have Patrols made lashings tight enough, have they been too economical on the amount of sisal used? A price should then be offered accordingly.
- If Patrols are not happy with the price offered it is down to them to change the buyer's opinion by selling features and pointing out the quality that may have gone unnoticed.

Note: You could choose to appoint one or more specialists - an 'advisor', 'supervisor', 'trainer', 'manager' or a 'negotiator' to get the best deal for your work. Try 'contracting' work to other Patrols or offering them part finished items to complete!

- Part way through the game allow Patrols the opportunity to create one item not on the finished end products list using any of the raw materials available.
- Patrols must buy materials from the trading post and use them to make items for resale to the store at a profit. (Only items based on the list can be purchased and sold.)
- Patrols must aim to make as much money as possible in the time allowed for the period of trading.
- Operations must be based on what Patrols think can work most effectively for them! Remember that 'time is money'!
- At the end of the playing period the Patrol's original 'financial loan' must be 'repaid' to the trading post.
- The Patrol that makes the greatest amount of profit wins.

Options for Trading Post

Equipment: As for previous game.
Players: Eight or more.

• The game could be designed to enable players to practice recently taught 'Scout' skills'.
• Lead a discussion on the outcome of the game in relation to problems that might be encountered in running a business in the real world.
• Discuss the topics of leadership and team-work especially around the questions of 'Is there value in having specialist roles?' 'Was anything learned that might be of value in working as a Patrol?'
• Try and relate this game to the difficulties faced by countries of the developing world in trading their goods on the world market.

INTERACTIVE GAMES

In the following games one Patrol member at a time competes against representatives from each of the other Patrols.

Dragstore

Equipment: One large rope upon which a string marker for each Patrol has been tied at equal intervals. A small object for each Patrol placed on a chair (or a marked position on the ground) behind each player.
Players: Twelve plus, divided into three teams.

• First, tie securely together the ends of the rope to form a large circle.
• 'Number off' within Patrols from the tallest down to the smallest.
• When a number is called e.g. *'two'*, the player corresponding to that number takes hold of the rope next to their Patrol marker. They may not move their hand(s) away from this marker during the game.
• On the signal *'start'*, player's try to pick up an object which has been positioned on a chair one metre behind them which belongs to the player either to their left or right and tries to place it next to their 'own' object.
• Players with two objects on the chair behind them score a point.
• The Patrol that scores the most points in the time allocated for the game wins.

Human Bowls

Equipment: A football (the 'jack'), one blindfold per Patrol.
Players: Six or more.

• Get the players to line up in Patrols at one end of the playing area and number off in ones and twos.
• The game leader kicks the ball - the 'jack' down field at the start of each new game, which is to be played in total silence.
• Player 'one' puts on the blindfold and walks to where they think the jack is and stops, whereupon they can remove the blindfold. When 'ones' have returned, 'twos' bowl themselves!
• Once players remove the blindfold they remain totally still. If a blindfolded player happens to touch someone then that player must stop. If this happens, the player is awarded a 'rebound' and may step one pace closer to the jack.
• The Patrol with the player judged to be nearest to the jack scores a point (two points for the nearest two players, etc.).
• The Patrol with the most points in the time allowed wins.

Sicilian Shove

Equipment: None.
Players: Six or more.

• Chalk or mark out a circle on the ground of the playing area and get the Patrols to number off accordingly.
• When a number is called out, corresponding members enter the circle and take hold of their own ankles with their hands, with the aim of trying to push all opponents out of the circle.
• If players let go of their ankles or touch the floor outside of the circle with any part of their body then they must sit out.
• Points are awarded to the last player left in the circle.
• The Patrol that scores the most points wins.

RACES

The following section contains games in which a Scout competes against other Scouts, either as an individual, or as Patrol members. Points are awarded to the individual or Patrol, at the end of each race before another set of Patrol representatives are selected to race off.

Most races can be turned into relays (see page 52) if, on completing the given activity, a player releases another Patrol member by tagging them. This continues until the whole team has completed the activity.

Unlike most other team games, races are not interactive and do not tend to involve teamwork or tactics. However they do enable players to demonstrate personal skills to themselves and others. Leaders can, therefore, use the games to test players either before or after training. For example, a race could be run to test knowledge of mapping symbols.

Activity Races

Equipment: As applicable (see below for examples).
Players: Any number.

• Patrols number off, ensuring every Patrol has equal numbers (it may be necessary for some players to have two numbers).
• Get all the players sitting down and cross legged.
• When a number is called out e.g. '*two*', the corresponding player leaves their Patrol and undertakes the given activity.
• Players who finish the activity first and return to the original sitting position win a point for their Patrol. The Patrol that scores the most points in the time allowed wins.

Dizzy

Equipment: As applicable, a bat or a stick.
Players: Any number.

• Players place their finger on the floor and revolve around it seven times (or just spin around) then walk a short course.
• Or, players could put one end of a bat or blunt stick on the ground and the other end touching their forehead before revolving around it seven times then walking a short course.
• Players who manage to walk the straightest line win points for their team.

Banana Race

Equipment: A banana for each player.
Players: Any number.

• Players must peel and eat a banana using only their left hand.
• A player is only finished once they can whistle.
• Points are awarded accordingly.

Pea And Paper

Equipment: A straw, dried peas or paper squares for each player, containers.
Players: Any number.

• Using a straw, players try transferring dried peas or paper squares from one container to another.
• Or, players must complete a short course carrying a dried pea or square using only a straw.
• The player who achieves this in the quickest time scores a point for their team. The team with the most points wins.

Theatre Race

Equipment: Various pieces of fancy dress.
Players: Any number.

• Run around a course whilst at the same time putting on and taking off fancy dress clothing.
• Points could be awarded for quickest dresser, undressed and finisher.

One-Two-Three-Four

Equipment: None.
Players: Any number.

• Touch all four walls of the room (relatively easy for those who think about it!).

Kangaroo Hop

Equipment: A ball for each Patrol.
Players: Any number.

• Mark out an obstacle course.
• Players try jumping around the course carrying a ball between their knees.
• The player who gets round the course in the quickest time without dropping the ball scores a point. A time penalty could be awarded for dropping the ball.

Training Races

Equipment: As applicable based on the examples below.
Players: Six or more.

- Players run a race which is completed only when they have tied a specific knot.
- Players run a race which is completed only when they have successfully put a sling on a patient.
- Players run a race which is completed only when they have successfully managed to put a person into the recovery position.
- Players run a race which is completed only when they have successfully identified either mapping symbols, leaves, constellations, flags, etc.
- Players run a race which is completed only when they have answered questions on a specific training topic.
- Players run a race which is completed only when they have successfully decoded a message.
- Players run a race which is completed only when they have correctly coiled a rope.
- Players run a race which is completed only when they have correctly thrown a coiled rope to hit a given target.
- Players run a race which is completed only when players can show they can successfully light a small fire (with the materials provided and under supervision).

Camel Races

Equipment: A die.
Players: As Patrols.

• In the playing area mark out a series of horizontal parallel lines one pace apart (or use markers).
• Get players to number off within their Patrols.
• Those players numbered 'one' stand in a row behind the first line and, in turn, throw the die. This is repeated by 'twos' and so on.
• If the number thrown corresponds to the same number as that of the player throwing it, they move forward one space.
• The player who crosses the finishing post first wins a point.
• The Patrol with the highest score once all players have had their turn is the winner.

Options for Camel Races

Equipment: A die, a difficult object to carry.
Players: As Patrols.

• Play the game as above, but get players to carry a difficult object between their knees or on their head (e.g. a cup of water).
• Players must go back a space if they drop the object.
• The player who crosses the finishing post first wins a point.
• This game could be played in Patrol heats, then have a Troop final.

RELAYS

Everybody is familiar with relays - you may have played a simple balloon relay during birthday celebrations when you were younger. The principal of any relay is that every member of a team completes one or more activity in a defined sequence. The first team to finish is normally the winner although the scoring could also take into account how well players complete their tasks, e.g. the number of correct answers, the volume of water carried, etc.

If so desired, relays can be made surprisingly complex by using different starting formations and introducing multiple level tasks. However, simple relays are usually exciting enough - both for participants and spectators alike. Unlike many games the team in the lead is nearly always identifiable and can easily change.

Relays can be played as a training exercise or purely for fun. In games in which individuals are 'on show' it is important to keep in tune with the feelings of players who have personal difficulties or special needs. Nobody likes to feel that they have let the side down.

There are four common relay formations used:
• Patrols in parallel files behind a real or imaginary line and facing the same direction. (A)
• Patrols standing one behind the other facing the centre. (B)
• Patrol circles, with players behind facing clockwise. (C)
• Patrol's split into two separate files at opposite ends of the playing area facing parallel to each other. (D)

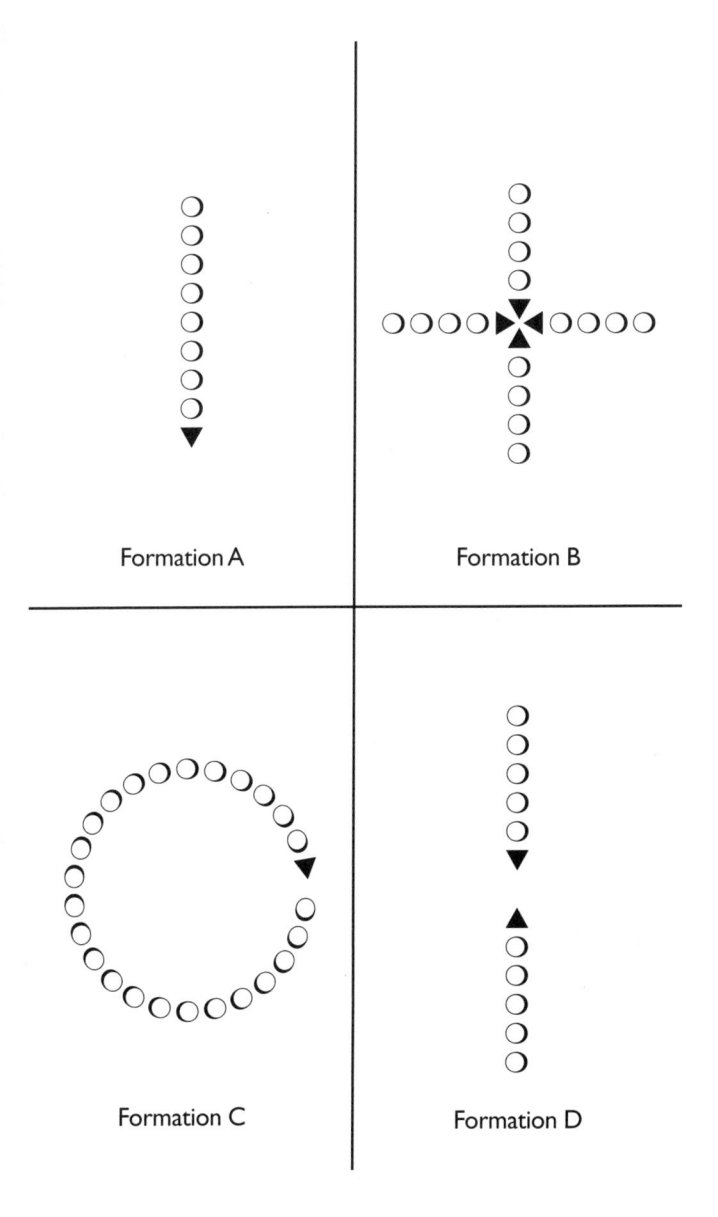

Formation A

Formation B

Formation C

Formation D

Classic Relay

Equipment: A rope, a chair.
Players: As Patrols.
Formation: A

• Set up a marker at the opposite end of the playing area away from the Patrols. For example, use a rope line, a chair, a wall or a Leader.
• Each player in turn races to the marker and back, undertaking an activity on the way to, from or at the marker (use an example from a past activity game).
• On returning to the starting position the next player is released by being tagged who then repeats the activity.
• When the last player has returned, everybody in the Patrol must sit down.
• The first Patrol to repeat the relay and sit down, wins.

Diagonal Relay

Equipment: A rope, a chair.
Players: As Patrols.
Formation: B

• Set up a marker in the centre of the playing area.
• Follow the instructions and play as for a regular relay game.
• The Leader, at the centre, gives players a task or question verbally or in writing, that they must answer before returning to tag the next player.
• When the last player has returned, everybody in the Patrol must sit down.
• The first Patrol to repeat the relay and sit down, wins.

Circle Relay

Equipment: An object for each Patrol.
Players: As Patrols.
Formation: C

• Start with a nominated player - number one, who must pass an object clockwise around the circle until it returns to them.
• Player number one then runs with the object around the circle returning back to their position and passes it forwards to the player in front - number two.
• Player number two passes the object a second time around the circle. (Once it is received players must run clockwise around the circle and back to their original place before passing the object forward to the next player and so on.)
• Once the final player (the player behind number one) has raced around the circle everyone sits down.
• The first Patrol to complete the relay and sit down is the winner.

Shuttle Relay

Equipment: An object for each Patrol.
Players: As Patrols.
Formation: D

• First, line up in Patrols and number off - one, two, etc.
• The first player in the Patrol line must race to the other end of the room and back tagging the next player in front of them - number two by passing them an object.
• Player number two passes the object a second time around the group. Once the object is received players run clockwise en route.
• The first Patrol to complete the relay and sit down wins.

Back Of The Queue

Equipment: An object if required.
Players: As Patrols.
Formation: A

• Undertake an activity - use one of the previous examples if you wish, but this time start with the back player first, playing through to the front player.
• Once the front player has completed the activity they race to the back of the queue tagging the next player or passing an object which may be part of the activity forwards again, and so on.
• The game carries on until players find themselves in their original starting order.
• The first Patrol to complete the relay and sit down is the winner.

Down The Line

Equipment: An object if required.
Players: As Patrols.
Formation: A

• Pass an object down the line until it reaches the final player or undertake an activity involving every player. (This race is applicable to activities that can not be achieved in any previous game.)
• Once the activity or object has reached or involved the final player everyone sits down.
• If a player drops the object return it to the front of the line and start again.
• The first Patrol to complete the race and sit down is the winner.

Water!

Equipment: Containers, water supply.
Players: As Patrols.

• Get the players to carry a full container of water, empty it into another container and pass the full container to the next player in relay fashion and so on.
• Or, get players to try to carry a container of water on their heads without the use of your hands.
• The team that passes the water from one end to the other with the least spillage is the winner.

Pass The Object

Equipment: Balloons, ball or a piece of fruit.
Players: As Patrols.

• Players try passing a balloon or ball to the next player using only their knees, head and shoulders or only their chests.
• Or, by passing a 'piece' of fruit without using their hands.
• The team that achieves this in the quickest time, wins.

Spoon Feeding

Equipment: String, spoons.
Players: As Patrols.

• First, tie a length of string to a spoon.
• The spoon should then be passed down through the outer garments of each player until they are all linked.
• The quickest team to link all its players is the winner.

Over And Under

Equipment: A football.
Players: As Patrols.

• In Patrols line up and number off in 'ones' and 'twos'.
• The first player - number one, passes the ball backwards overhead to the second player who then passes the ball between their legs and so on, until everyone has passed the ball on.
• The team that passes the ball to the back of their team the quickest is the winner.

Elephant Relay

Equipment: None.
Players: As Patrols.
Formation: D

• Starting with the first player in line at one end of the room, race to the other end of the play area.
• 'Pick- up' the player at the front of the line as per the instructions by standing in front of the player and passing your left hand between your legs (from the front). Use this hand to hold the right hand of the player behind.
• As a twosome go to the other end of the room and pick up another player who joins on at the back of the twosome.
• Once you have picked up and returned with all the players sit down.
• The first Patrol to complete the relay and sit down is the winner.

Staves

Equipment: One stave per Patrol or team.
Players: As Patrols.
Formation: A

- Players number off accordingly down the line.
- Player number one should turn around and face the rest of the Patrol.
- Holding the stave horizontally with both hands they throw the stave to player number two.
- After player number two has caught the stave with both hands it must be thrown back to player one, horizontally, after which player two crouches down with their hands over their head.
- Player one then throws the stave over the seated player to player three and so on.
- Once the last player in the line up returns the stave they then tap the shoulder of the player in front of them, who must then stand up to receive the stave again.
- This should continue down the line until all the Patrol has caught and thrown the stave at least twice.

Message Relay

Equipment: 10-15 words of 'instruction' written on pieces of paper and placed in a separate container for each Patrol.
Players: As Patrols.

- Taking it in turns, each player runs up and collects a word from their Patrol's container, returning with it to base or by memorising it.
- The collected words need to be arranged to give you the 'instruction'.
- The first Patrol to carry out the 'instruction' is the winner.

Rucsac Relay

Equipment: Each Patrol will need a rucsac and typical personal equipment for either a camp or hike.
Players: As Patrols.
Formation: A

• Place the empty rucsac at the opposite end of the room from the Patrols.
• Place the personal items to be packed directly in front of each Patrol.
• Each Player, in turn, selects an item, packs it in the rucsac and returns to their Patrol.
• Points should be awarded according to how well the rucsac is packed and the time taken. Therefore it is important that Patrols think about the order in which they pack items.
• The Patrol with the most points is the winner.

Tips: Equipment might include a drinking container, clothes, a map and compass, first aid kit, boots, sleeping bag and a dustbin liner - see how many Patrols think of putting this item in first to line their rucsac. Heavy items as a rule should be packed on top. However it is also important that certain items should be easily retrievable. Test this out by running races to see how quickly such items can be retrieved. You could do this by posing various circumstances - 'It is pouring with rain', 'Somebody has badly cut a finger', 'You need a drink', 'You need protection from the sun's rays', etc.

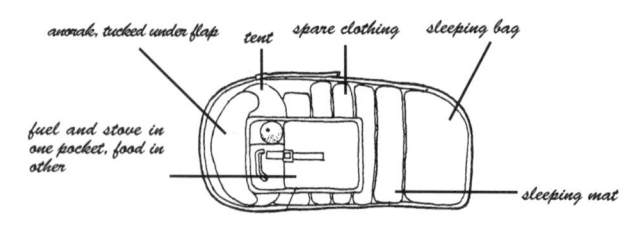

anorak, tucked under flap — *tent* — *spare clothing* — *sleeping bag*

fuel and stove in one pocket, food in other

sleeping mat

Human Clock Relay

Equipment: A ball.
Players: 10 or more plus.

- Divide the players into two teams - A and B.
- Team A (the relay team) should stand in a file (one behind each other) at one end of the room or play area and carry out a relay activity (choose from the previous examples).
- The second team - B (the human clock) forms a standing circle with one of its players in the centre.
- A ball should be passed back and forth between the centre player and the players in the circle. This should be done in a clockwise direction.
- Team B should try to achieve as many passes as possible in the time it takes for team A to complete their relay. (A pass equals the number of times that the ball is returned to the centre player.)
- Both teams then swap over their activity.
- The relay team that completes the activity in the fastest time as measured by the human clock, wins.

Whirling Wheel

Equipment: One object per Patrol (e.g. a ball or beanbag) together with cones to mark the circumference of the circle.
Players: As Patrols.
Formation: B, except that Patrol lines move forward to the centre as if they were spokes of a wheel.

- Place the beanbag or whatever your object is at the hub (centre) of the 'wheel'.
- The front player should pick up the object, run down the right hand side of their Patrol, around the last player, then

clockwise around the 'wheel' and back to the end of the Patrol's line.
• This is followed by passing the object from player to player down the line. Do not throw it.
• Once the object reaches the new front player the exercise should be repeated.
• The first Patrol to complete the relay and sit down is the winner.

Trust Your Guide

Equipment: Objects to be used as markers.
Players: As Patrols.

• Patrol teams should number off into ones and twos.
• Mark off a start line across one end of the playing area and place markers (e.g. chairs) at the other end, one opposite each team.
• Get player number one to choose any two players from their team.
• Player one then stands at the starting line facing the far marker. The two chosen players should stand either side of player one, who faces the opposite direction and link arms with them.
• On the signal '*start*' player one races around the far end marker and back, whilst at the same time acting as guide to the players next to them who must walk backwards and are not allowed to look in the direction in which they are travelling.
• Once player one crosses the line, they 'tag' to release player two. (Note: each 'guide' must choose a new pair of players.)
• The first team to complete the relay and sit down is the winner.

Transfer Relay

Equipment: One empty container per team, objects such as balls, beanbags or similar (one per team plus one extra) stored in a central container.
Players: As Patrols.
Formation: B

• First, place the empty containers approximately seven paces away from the central container so they are an equal distance apart from each other.
• Patrols should then form a queue seated behind their allocated empty container.
• On the signal '*start*', the first player stands up, collects one object and transfers it to their Patrol's container. (Objects can be taken from the central or from another Patrol's container.)
• The Player returns and 'tags' to release the next player in line before taking their place at the back of the queue.
• The first Patrol to get three objects in its container simultaneously is the winner (Try four objects if this is too easy!).

Weavers Relay

Equipment: None.
Players: As Patrols.
Formation: C

• First, get the Patrols to form standing circles.
• On the signal '*start*' the first player weaves in and out of the other players in a clockwise direction around the circle.
• Once they have returned to their place they must tag the player in front who repeats the activity, and so on.
• The first Patrol to complete the relay and sit down is the winner.

SPORTING GAMES

This section is devoted to games of a sporting nature and includes variations of popular team games such as football, cricket and rounders. Such games are sometimes referred to as 'field games' although many of them can be adapted to suit indoor conditions.

Therefore before you start you will need to decide:
• What object to use e.g. a football, flying disc, balloon or rugby ball.
• What type of goal to adopt e.g. a set of posts, a line, a hoop or a hole.
• How possession can be obtained e.g. tackling, intercepting or tagging.
• What passing methods to adopt, e.g. throwing, kicking, hitting or volleying.
• Rules for holding possession and passing, e.g. no running with the object, backward passing only and applying the off-side rule.
• How to define the scoring of a goal, e.g. the object must cross a line, the object and player must cross a line together, the player must touch the goal with the object, or the player must catch the ball whilst standing in the designated goal area.

The Score-switch Rule
When playing any goal-scoring game it can be difficult to achieve balanced sides. To avoid one-sided games try the 'Score-switch' rule which means any player who scores a goal moves to the opposing team.

Long Goal

Equipment: A football.
Players: 12 or more - divided in two equal teams.

• Mark a line behind each team (or use end walls if playing indoors).
• Divide the players into two teams who stand facing each other across a line marked off in the centre of the playing area. Teams should be approximately five - ten paces apart.
• Get teams to number off down their line from the left.
• Numbers 'one', 'two' and 'three' from each team go into the area between the teams and play handball, three against three.
• The remaining players on each team link arms and must defend their 'goal' (the line or wall) behind them. Defending teams are allowed to move from side to side to block shots from the opposition.
• When the game leader calls '*change*' player four (who is situated on the left-hand side of the line) must replace player one who rejoins the line at the right-hand end.
• Then on the next call of '*change*' player five will replace player two and so on.
• Players score by trying to hit the opponent's goal by passing the ball through or around their defensive wall.
• Any shots passing above shoulder height are disallowed.
• Players must not move with the ball or try to kick it. The ball may only be handled with one hand at a time.
• The team which scores the most goals in the time allowed is the winner.

Knock-out

Equipment: A football (or as appropriate), a single goal area.
Players: Six or more.

• Mark out the playing area and divide players either into small groups or let them play as individuals games like football etc.
• As soon as a player scores a goal they must 'sit out' as they have progressed to the next round.
• The last player left must then drop out of the game.
• The other players return for the second round at the end of which a further player must drop out too.
• The rounds continue until just two players are left to compete in the final round.
• The player who scores first in the final round is the winner.
Tip: An ideal spare time game for small groups. This idea can be applied to most popular goal scoring games which are played in knock-out rounds.

Target Ball

Equipment: A target for each team such as a tree or rope circle, a ball (alternatively use a flying disc or balloon).
Players: Six or more.

• First, divide the players into two or more teams.
• At the start of the game, or to restart the game after a goal has been scored, the game leader will throw the ball randomly into the centre of the playing area.
• A goal will be awarded each time a team successfully hits their own target with the ball, flying disc or balloon.
• Players score by either kicking the object or by throwing it.
• No physical contact is allowed or running with the object at any time.
• The team which scores the most goals in the time allowed, wins.

Variations on Target Ball

- Use a single central target.
- Allow the ball to be kicked but not thrown (or vice versa).
- Introduce tagging whereby the ball must be released immediately if a person is tagged.

Multi-team Football

Equipment: One football per team, one goal per team.
Players: Nine or more, divided into three teams.

- First, divide players into teams.
- Create a circular playing area - a 'pitch' where the goals should be an equal distance apart and face the centre of the pitch.
- Each team has to defend their allocated goal.
- On the signal '*start*' teams 'kick-off' in front of their own goal and attempt to score in any of the opponents' goals using any of the balls in play.
- No goalkeepers are allowed i.e. the ball can not be handled, and a maximum of two members from a team may defend their own goal at any one time. These players are allowed to be changed at any time.
- Nominated score keepers behind each goal should keep a record of the goals conceded by each team.
- If a goal is scored, or when the ball goes out of play, the nearest score keeper should throw the ball 'back-in' towards the centre of the pitch.
- The team which concedes the least amount of goals during the agreed playing time is the winner.

Roll Ball

Equipment: A light weight football, approximately one tennis ball per player.
Players: Eight or more.

- Mark out two parallel lines about five - ten paces apart across the centre of the playing area, and place the ball there.
- Divide the players into two teams who then stand behind a respective allocated line.
- The teams must try to score a goal by bombarding the football with tennis balls until it crosses their opponents' line.
- Teams must always remain behind their lines and throw all balls under-arm. Any tennis balls that stop between the lines should be retrieved by the game leader and returned to their respective team.
- The team which scores the most goals in the time allowed is the winner.

Penguin Ball

Equipment: None.
Players: Six or more.

- Mark out two 'goal' lines at opposite ends of the playing area.
- Divide the players into two teams with each team allocated a playing half.
- The game leader stands in the middle and becomes the game 'ball'.
- A goal is scored every time the leader is pushed across each team's opponent's goal line.
- The team which scores the most 'goals' in the time allowed wins.

Goal Catcher (Tower Ball)

Equipment: One ball, two chairs.
Players: Eight or more.

• Set the two chairs up, one at either end of the playing area.
• Divide the players into two teams who stand in opposite halves of the playing area.
• A nominated member from each team stands on the chair 'upfield'. This player is the 'goal-catcher'.
• The teams move around the playing area vying with their opponents for the best attacking and defending positions.
• When the game leader shouts '*Stop*', players must remain exactly where they are, whereupon the ball will be thrown 'blindly' into the centre of play by the game leader using a backwards overhead throw.
• A goal is only scored if the ball is passed between several members of a team until it can be successfully caught by their goal catcher.
• Once a goal has been scored players have a few seconds to choose a new position and the game commences as before.
• After two successful catches the goal-catcher must be changed.
• The team which scores the most goals during the game wins.

Box Ball

Equipment: A ball (alternatively use a flying disc or balloon).
Players: Eight or more.

• Mark out a box (approximately two metres by two metres) on the ground at either end of the playing area.
• Divide the players into two teams.
The game starts or 'throws-off' and restarts after a goal from the centre spot.

- Each team passes the ball towards the goal by throwing it to other members of their team. Players must not at anytime move with the ball.
- Possession can be gained from the other team by trying to intercept their throws but no physical contact is allowed between players.
- To score a goal the ball must be caught by any member from the same team whilst standing in the box up-field. A player must have both feet inside the box when the ball is caught for it to count.
- Players may not stand in the box for more than five seconds and can not return to it until another player from their team has stepped outside - so there is no 'goal hanging!'
- Teams can only defend around their own box and must not obstruct any player who wishes to enter.
- An obstruction will result in a penalty.
- To take a penalty, the ball is thrown from a distance of ten paces to a player waiting in the box to catch it.
- The team that scores the most goals at the end of the agreed playing time is the winner.
- For a variation use a single central target instead of two end zones or introduce tagging whereby the ball must be released immediately if a player is tagged.

Touch Rugby

Equipment: A rugby ball or football.
Players: Eight or more.

- Mark out a line across opposite ends of the playing area (or use end walls if playing indoors).
- Divide players into two teams which occupy opposite halves of the playing area.
- Players are allowed to run with the ball and must pass it backwards as soon as they are 'touched'.

- The ball is transferred to the other team if the game leader judges that a forward pass has been made or if the ball has not been released straight away.
- The ball can be won through players from each team intercepting passes, although no tackling of any kind is allowed.
- Teams are awarded one point for each 'touch-down' i.e. when the ball is 'touched' into the opposite end past the marker line by any attacking player.
- The team which scores the most points in the time allowed wins.

Tripod Football (Multi-team)

Equipment: A football, a tripod of three staves per team (or any object that can be easily knocked over).
Players: Four or more.

- Set up a goal for each team an equal distance apart by resting three staves (or any other object) together in the form of a tripod in such a way that the slightest touch will knock the structure over.
- Divide players into Patrol teams containing about four or five players.
- Each player from each team takes it in turns to knock down an opponent's tripod using the football to score a point.
- If a player knocks their own team's tripod over, a point is deducted from their team's final total.
- The team with the most points at the end of the agreed playing time is the winner.
- As a variation play with just two teams and a single central tripod.
- One of the teams attacks and tries to knock over the tripod with the ball, whilst the other team defends. Change attackers and defenders over after an agreed period of time.

Team Pass Football

Equipment: A football (or flying disc, balloon or tennis ball).
Players: Six or more.

• Divide into teams of about five or six players.
• To start the game, or to restart after a goal has been scored, the game leader will throw the football (or flying disc, balloon or tennis ball) randomly into the centre of the playing area.
• As there are no goal posts in this game, a goal is awarded by continuously and successfully passing the ball to each member of your team without losing it to the opposing team.
• The team which scores the most 'goals' (passes) in the time allowed wins the game.

Flying Disc Golf

Equipment: A flying disc or plastic plate per player; a number of large flat objects (sacks or roll mats are ideal).
Players: Four or more.

• First, position the chosen objects across the playing area and number them accordingly.
• Players then go around the 'course' in small teams as if they were playing a round of golf. The objects in this game represent 'holes'.
• In turns, players throw their flying discs as many times as necessary until they finally come to rest touching a 'hole'.
• Players throw the flying disc towards each new hole from the previous one.
• Each player should note down their score - the number of throws it has taken, at the end of each hole.
• The player with the lowest total score at the end of the 'course' wins.

Double Football

Equipment: A football.
Players: Eight or more.

• Mark out a football pitch on the playing area.
• Divide the players into two equal teams.
• This game should be played along the lines of conventional football but use two balls and two referees for each team.
• Identify for each team which goals they need to defend and which ones they need to attack.

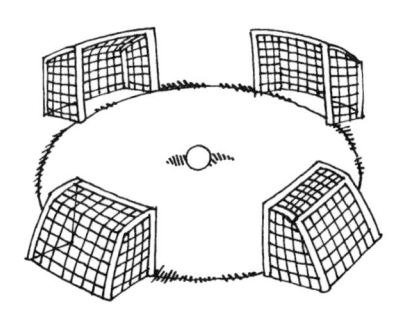

• Each team must attack and defend at the same time. Note there is no offside rule in this game.
• The team that scores more goals than it concedes is the winner.

RUN-SCORING GAMES

The aim of this type of game is to score points by running between two bases, lines or wickets. The number of runs achieved depends upon the skill with which an object, usually a ball, is hit, kicked or thrown. It is also determined by the bowling and fielding skills of the opposing team. Cricket is possibly the best known example of this type of game.

Before starting a game it is important that each player knows:
• How many attempts at a 'strike' will be allowed before a run must be made.
• Whether a run must be made even if the ball is not hit.
• When or whether a bowled ball will be classed as a 'no-ball'. (It is common practice to disallow any ball that does not reach the batter at a height between the shoulder and knee.)
• Whether any special rules apply if the ball is hit behind.
Note: A disadvantage with batting games is that players who become 'out' early on may have to endure a long period of inactivity. Consider applying the 'all-out' rule (see below). Alternatively devise rules that allow players to rejoin the game after a certain period of time has elapsed.

The 'All-out' Rule
By applying this rule the whole batting team will be 'out' if the ball is caught by a fielder. The rule usually results in teams playing more but shorter 'innings' which keeps the game moving. It also means that players who become 'out' may still get further opportunities to bat. It is a good idea to establish a fixed batting order to ensure fair batting opportunities across the team. Recommence each new innings with the player who was due to bat when the last innings ended.

Drop Ball

Equipment: Bat and ball.
Players: 12 or more.

• Mark out two parallel lines (A and B) on the playing area, ideally they should be at least 25 paces apart.
• Divide the players into two teams - 'batters' and 'fielders'.
• The team of batters stands behind line A. Each player takes a turn to bat whereby they move forward and stand anywhere on the line.
• The batter then throws the ball into the air, above head height and attempts to hit it as it descends.
• Whether the batter hits the ball or not, they must try to run towards line B. If, and when, they cross line B, they can either return straight away to line A or wait and return later on after any other of their team members' strikes.
• Once a batter returns to line A a point is scored, and they then return to the back of the queue for another go.
• The fielders must try to get the batting team 'out' as quickly as possible to keep the batters' score to a minimum. A batter is out if a 'strike' is caught, if they are hit with the ball whilst running between the lines and if a batter is located anywhere other than behind line A when another member of their team is 'got' out.
• Fielders are not allowed to run with the ball. (It is usually more effective to pass the ball between players than to attempt a long range throw.)
• Teams should swap roles when there are no more players left to bat.
• The team which scores the greatest number of runs wins.
• As a variation try drop kicking a football instead of batting a ball or get bowler's to roll or throw a ball to the batter.

No Bowler Cricket

Equipment: Cricket bat, tennis ball and stumps (or something equivalent).
Players: Six or more.

• Mark out the playing area to resemble a cricket pitch - remember it is oval in shape.
• Divide all the players into two equal teams.
• The game should be played along the lines of conventional cricket but without a bowler!
• To bat the player must balance the ball on the flat side of the bat, flip the ball into the air and then try to hit it.
• Even if a player misses the ball they must attempt to make a run.
• The team which scores the greatest number of runs wins.

Big Kick

Equipment: A football.
Players: Eight or more.

• In the playing area mark out two bases between 10 and 15 paces apart which should be connected by a marked channel, three paces wide.
• Divide the players into two teams - 'strikers' and 'fielders'. who after an agreed time swap over.
• The team of strikers, assembles at one of the bases known as the kicking base and in turn, 'drop kicks' the football.
• When the ball has been kicked strikers must run to the other base and back as many times as possible until they have all been struck below the knee with the ball. (A run equals one completed returned run.)
• The team of fielders must use the strikers' kicked ball to get

them out as quickly as possible by hitting the striker below the knee with it. However, fielders may not move whilst they have possession of the ball or enter the channel between bases.
• If a fielder catches the ball directly from a kick, the striker is not out but the whole striking team looses five runs.
• The team scoring the greatest number of runs is the winner.

Continuous Cricket

Equipment: Cricket bat, tennis ball and stumps (or something equivalent).
Players: Eight or more.

• Set up a wicket, a stump to mark the bowling position and a stump at the square leg position (five - ten paces to the left of the batsman, at right angles to the line of bowling).
• Divide players into two equal teams. One team bats whilst the other fields.
• Players from the batting team whether they hit the ball or not, must try to run around the square leg stump and back to the wicket before they are bowled or caught out during their run to score a point. (Make sure the batter drops the bat before running.)
• As soon as one batter is out the new batter must get to the crease as quickly as possible. As this is continuous cricket the bowler will not wait for them to take their position!
• The fielders must get the ball back to their bowler as quickly as possible who can then bowl as soon as the ball is returned whether the batter is at the striking crease or not to defend the wicket.
• Batters are 'out' if they are caught or bowled. They can not be stumped or run out.
• The teams should change over after an agreed period of time or when the batting team are all 'out'.
• The team which scores the most runs in its 'innings', wins.

Throw Home

Equipment: A bat and ball, a wicket e.g. three stumps or a large container.
Players: Six or more.

- Mark out the playing area and set up a 'wicket'.
- Divide players into two equal teams - 'batters' and 'fielders'.
- Players from the batting team, in turn, stand in front of the wicket and attempt to hit the bowled ball.
- Batters are allowed three attempts to hit the ball but on the first successful hit they step aside so that fielders have an 'open' wicket.
- Once there is an 'open' wicket fielders aim to hit the wicket in the minimum number of throws.
- Fielders can change positions prior to the ball being struck but once the ball is struck can only move if they are in a position to catch the ball or if they are the closest fielder to the ball.
- Once a fielder has possession they remain rooted to the spot and call out the name of another fielder. Only this fielder may move to field their throw. Once the ball is collected, this fielder must stop and select another fielder and so on.
- A batter will be out if the ball is caught or if a fielder can hit the wicket directly from the spot where the ball is first fielded from.
- If a batter successfully makes a strike they return to the batting queue.
- The batter scores runs according to the number of throws it takes fielders to hit the wicket with the ball.
- Teams should swap over after an agreed time.
- The team which scores the greatest number of runs is the winner.
- A variation on this game could be that the batter drop kicks a football or that fielders may kick but not throw the ball.

SCORING ROUNDERS

The previous section dealt with run-scoring games in which runs are accumulated by running between two fixed bases. Rounders and its variations differ only in that points are awarded by running to a *series* of bases. Conventionally batters run around the bases in an anti-clockwise direction. Smaller Troops can play many of the these games by allowing each Scout to compete individually against the rest of the Troop, and by recording their own score.

Before playing you will need to determine the following:
• Whether the striker must run on the first, second or third attempted strike or, on any strike when contact is made with the ball.
• Whether a player who hits the ball behind may or may not run beyond the first base.
• If any member of the batting team can or can not be got 'out' by being struck below the knee with the ball whilst running between bases.
• Whether you consider a base to be stumped if a fielder throws the ball and makes a direct hit, if the ball is placed on the base directly by a fielder, or if the fielder touches the base whilst holding the ball, i.e. a fielder may stand on the base and simply catch the ball to stump it.
• Whether a player is to be considered 'out' if they have started out towards a base that has been or becomes stumped; or is more than halfway towards a base that has been, or becomes, stumped.
• If players can or can not continue to run beyond the next base once the the bowler has the ball.
• The 'all-out' rule is or is not applied.

Triangular Rounders

Equipment: A football.
Players: Eight or more.

• Divide the players into two teams - 'strikers' and 'fielders'.
• Set up three bases forming a triangle and mark a spot from where the football will be kicked, approximately ten metres from the triangle, mid-way between the first and last base.
• Then play the game as you would for conventional rounders except that strikers should, from the marked spot, kick the ball into or across the triangular area formed by the three bases. (Make sure all the players are familiar with the rules you adopt for playing the game.)
• The fielding team must, before each strike, stand outside the triangle until the ball is kicked.
• The teams should swap over after an agreed time.
• The team that scores the most 'rounds' is the winner.
(This version of rounders is ideal for small groups and confined spaces.)

Flying Disc Base

Equipment: A flying disc, base markers.
Players: Eight or more.

• Mark out four bases in the shape of an equilateral diamond approximately 10 metres long x 10 metres wide.
• Select one of the bases to become the 'throwing point'.
• Number anti-clockwise the other bases 'one', 'two' and 'three' from this base. The throwing point should be chosen so that all players who throw from it face base two with their backs to the wind.
• Divide the players into two teams - 'fielders' and 'throwers'.

• The throwers line up and, in turn, throw the flying disc from the throwing point. After they launch the flying disc players must start to run anti-clockwise around the bases back towards the start.

• Only one throw is permitted at a time and no stopping at bases in between is allowed.

• If players make it back to the throwing base they score five points and may immediately throw again. A thrower can also score one, two or three points according to the highest numbered base reached before they are out.

• The fielders attempt to get the thrower out by catching the flying disc or by touching the thrower whilst holding it.

• If the flying disc lands behind the first base then the thrower is also out.

• Change sides at the mid-point of the game so that each team has an equal innings. Once a player is out they rejoin the throwing queue.

• The team that scores the most points in the time allowed is the winner.

Crazy Rounders

Equipment: Bat and ball.
Players: Eight or more.

• Set out about ten randomly positioned bases, numbered from one upwards. Make sure you show players the location of each base and allow them time to learn the sequential course from base to base.

• Mark out striking and bowling positions.

• Divide players into two teams - 'batters and 'fielders'.

• Batters must run in numerical order from base to base on their first attempted hit, leaving the bat behind.

• Batters may choose to halt their initial run at any of the bases and will score points according to the number of the

base reached (e.g. four points if they reach base four).
- Batters are 'out' if their next base is stumped whilst they are between bases or if the ball hit is caught. No points are scored if they are caught or stumped on their initial run.
- As soon as any batsman attempts to hit the ball those players positioned on bases can continue around the course. They will not score points for those bases reached after their initial run but if they successfully complete the course without becoming 'out' they are allowed to bat again. (Note: At no time can there be more than one batter on any one base.)
- The team fielding should spread out in fielding positions of their choosing.
- Bowling, underarm, the bowler aims to stump or catch out players of the opposing side.
- If a *no ball* (a ball that does not reach the batter between shoulder and knee height) is called they may continue running or choose to take a strike again.
- The innings end when there are no more available batters.
- The team with the highest scoring innings is the winner.
- A variation on this game could be to agree on a set time limit for each innings.
- Players are 'out' if they are hit by the ball between bases.
- Players are 'out' by being touched by a fielder holding the ball whilst between bases.
- Tip: Depending upon the number of players in each team relative to the number of bases, it may not be practical, or even possible, to have an allocated fielder for each base. Therefore fielders will need to move around more than in conventional rounders to ensure that appropriate bases are covered according to the changing circumstances.

Indoor Rounders

Equipment: Soft ball, a bat.
Players: Eight or more.

- Mark out four bases and striking and bowling positions within the playing area.
- Divide players into two teams - 'strikers' and 'fielders', get the striking team to number off to establish an order of batting.
- Except for the first batter, both teams take up fielding positions around the room. Once in position no player may move from their spot. The penalty for disobeying this rule is a rounder to the other team.
- The batter has to run on their first hit and attempt to score a rounder by touching all four bases (the four corners of the room if you like). Unlike conventional rounders you can not stop off at a base. After scoring a rounder the batter strikes again until they are finally out.
- If the ball comes within reach of the batter whilst running around the bases, they may knock it away from the reach of the opposing team. However they may not throw the ball or attempt to keep it (i.e. they must knock it on immediately).
- The team fielding must attempt to get members of the batting team 'out' by catching their hits (including catches off the wall or ceiling) or by throwing the ball to the bowler, either directly or via other members of their team. But unlike conventional rounders you can not stump players out at bases.
- Fielders are, however, allowed to jump up for high balls so long as they land on the same spot.
- The individual or team (depending on how you wish to play) with the most rounders is the winner.

WIDE GAMES

A wide game is basically a game played over a wide area. This can either be in a park, field, at a camp site or in a wooded area, across open countryside or around your local community - though preferably somewhere secure and with an easily definable boundary thus preventing players from wandering off too far.

In the early days of Scouting exercises over wide areas were commonly known as 'Field Days' - a term that held military connotations. The exercises could take place across several miles and last for most of a day. The modern wide game is usually somewhat less ambitious. All of the games detailed in this section can be played in about 45-90 minutes and within one square kilometre. This can make them suitable as an activity for a Troop night. With good planning, back-up support and time on your side there is no reason why these games can not be extended further afield. Troop camps for example, would provide an ideal opportunity.

Types of wide games and their aims
- Cordon-breaking - getting through a guarded cordon, usually to deliver a message or items from one location to another.
- Man-hunt - to locate a person or persons.
- Treasure hunt - to find clues and/or treasure.
- Raid - to raid an opponent's base(s) whilst at the same time defending one's own and/or to obtain 'lives' whilst protecting one's own 'life'.

Note: Some wide games are a combination of two or more of the above types.

Skills
Wide games can demand a variety of skills from players - imagination, teamwork, planning, cunning, ingenuity and patience. If wide games are fairly new to your Troop do not be surprised if they have only limited appeal at first - it can take time for a Troop to develop the skills and attitude needed to enjoy wide games to the full.

Instructions and rules
It is important to ensure that instructions and rules are understood before starting. It is often helpful to give out written instructions and to allow a short period before starting the game to allow teams to work out a strategy - their 'game plan'.

Using wide games as a training tool
Wide games can help develop leadership, teamwork and planning skills. They also provide an obvious opportunity for map and compass work. By adding 'incidents' to games players can be provided with an opportunity to 'field test' skills that they may have learned in the headquarters - first aid, communication, cooking, pioneering and rope-work are good examples.

'Pieces'
Most cordon-breaking games involve the smuggling of objects past guards. For the purpose of this publication such items have simply been referred to as 'pieces'. You can use items such as cardboard chits (biodegradable when dropped!), plastic counters, pieces of aluminium foil, cups of water or sweets. Through the magic of wide games such items might become gold bullion, rocket fuel, computer chips, a vital antidote - the list is as long as your imagination! Alternatively, 'pieces' could be sections of a message or real items of equipment (staves, sisal, etc.) which are to be assembled together in a safe area past the cordon of guards.

'Lives'
A 'life' is an article, worn or carried, that allows a player to participate in the game. If a 'life' is lost then the player must drop out or return to base to get a new one! In cordon-breaking games the 'piece' being carried usually doubles up as a 'life'. In other games a 'life' might be a stave, a length of sisal hanging loosely from a belt like a tail or a woollen armband that breaks when 'snatched'.

Methods of obtaining a life from a player
• Firstly through 'tag and give'. Tagged players must automatically hand over their 'life'
• 'Tag and find'. Tagged players must allow a one minute search for their 'life'. The 'life' may be hidden anywhere on the player except beneath undergarments.
• 'Tag and challenge'. Tagged players are challenged and must hand over their 'life' if they lose. The challenge could take the form of a duel (see page 19). Alternatively each player could carry a numbered card, whereby the player holding the lowest card loses.
• A life can be 'snatched' from a player. This is only applicable for loose or easily breakable 'lives' (e.g. hats, woollen armbands or string tails). Note: It is important to prevent excessive force being used in the taking or protection of a life. The best procedure to adopt is to disallow all physical contact other than blocking.

Safety
Wide games, by their very nature, do not usually involve close supervision by adult Leaders. Indeed, part of the very attraction and benefit of wide games is the responsibility given to Members to leave the headquarters and work matters out unassisted. In accepting this responsibility a team must recognise the importance of looking after their own safety.

Safety checklist for wide game participants
Below are listed important factors that must be considered and understood before undertaking the playing of wide games.
• If there is an accident or an incident will Leaders be able to get adequate help quickly?
• It is important that support is available and that players know how to get hold of it. For a small wide game this could entail a Leader left at a central base. For games that go further afield it is advisable to carry written details of emergency telephone numbers and contact locations. If help is only available from a location which, for the purposes of the game, is intended to be secret, then details could be provided by the game leader in a sealed envelope for players to open only in the event of an emergency. Mobile phones are not only a valuable safety tool but they open up a whole new variety of game possibilities - phoning in answers, issuing out the next set of instructions, etc.
• Do players have all the equipment that they need? For games that are relatively local little or no specific equipment is usually required. For wider based games consider taking the following - first aid kit, adequate food and drink, waterproofs, suitable warm clothing and adequate sun protection, torches, money for an emergency call and emergency whistles.
• Make sure that all medical needs can be met while you are away from base e.g. access to prescribed medication, asthma ventilares, etc. It is recommended that players wear their Scout neckerchief for any games outside of the camp or headquarter's boundaries.
• Is there an appropriate level of expertise in each team? This depends on the task and location. For a small woodland game at a camp site youngsters can safely play as individuals. For wider games teams of five to eight players are appropriate. Ensure that all members of each team know the importance of staying together.
• Do players know where they can and can not go?

- Boundaries and 'no go' areas should be explained to everyone playing before a game starts.
- If a player loses their way will they be able to find their way back?
- If the game is being played outside in an unfamiliar area then teams should take maps and compasses with them.
- For games in which players are involved in 'hunting' for bases or locating them from descriptions, it is recommended that players or teams should carry sealed envelopes containing information to assist them if they lose their way.
- Make sure all players know the time when they must return. It is important that all players appreciate the difficulties that can be caused by arriving back late.

Storylines

A wide game can be enlivened by giving it a theme, a storyline and make-believe locations, characters and equipment. The opportunities are only as limited as your imagination! A few suggestions are provided below.

Robin Hood (example)

- Locations - Nottingham castle, Sherwood forest.
- Characters - Robin Hood and his merry men, the Sheriff of Nottingham's men, Maid Marion, Friar Tuck.
- Themes - robbing the rich to give to the poor, Robin and Little John's battle to ford a river from opposite sides, the rescuing of Maid Marion.
- 'Pieces' represent arrows, rope, money.

Star Trek (example)

• Locations - the planets and galaxies e.g. Vulcan, or Andoria; Star Fleet Command Headquarters, areas of the USS Enterprise e.g. the bridge, sick bay and the transporter room.
• Characters - USS Enterprise crew; Fleet Command; the United Federation of Planets (formed in 2161 to ensure that all beings through the galaxies coexist peacefully); teams could choose from a host of inter-galactic races such as *Xepolites* (free traders), *Ferengi* (only interested in profit), *Miradorn* (Raiders), *Klingons* (nomadic warriors), *Vulcans* (do not show emotions), *Breen* (secretive), *Romulans* (spread out across the galaxies) and *Andorians* (intelligent blue skinned race).
• Themes - seeking out new civilisations, ensuring peaceful coexistence of all the races in the galaxies.
• 'Pieces' represent transporter power, items of trade between races, starship components - crystals to generate warp speed, space miles!

Environmental (example)

• Locations - the developing world, rain forests, city streets, a player's local town!
• Characters - trees, foresters, governments, charity workers, medics, industry, countries of the developing world, 'Western' countries.
• Themes - stopping pollution, preventing litter, saving the rain forest, raising awareness of global warming, stopping graffiti artists, feeding the planet's hungry people, providing water.
• 'Pieces' represent money, medical supplies, food, water, pollution, trees, litter.

King Arthur And The Round Table

- Locations - Camelot, the Round Table, the Isle of Avalon (Arthur's historic seat).
- Characters - King Arthur, Uther Pendragon (father), Queen Guinevere, Merlin the Magician, the knights of the Round Table e.g. Sir Lancelot du Lac, Sir Robin, Sir Hector, Sir Galahad, Sir Percival, Sir Bedivere and Sir Lionel.
- Themes - the chivalrous conduct of the knights (see *Scouting for Boys* by Baden-Powell), jousting tournaments between knights, defeating the Saxons, pulling the sword from a stone to be proclaimed King of all Britain, obtaining Excalibur (Arthur's trusted sword given to him out of the water by the mysterious lady of the lake), pilgrimages of the knights to the Holy Land, searching for the Holy Grail.
- 'Pieces' - represent the elements of a knight's training (link it to B.-P.'s concept for Scouting, the Scout Law and Promise), pieces of a knight's armour, articles for Merlin's spells, etc.

The Vikings And Alfred The Great

- Locations - Danelaw (that part of Britain under Viking rule), villages of the ancient Britons (find out the names of ancient villages that existed in your local area. Look for endings such as... -by, -dale, -fell, -thorpe and -wick).
- Characters - Vikings, ancient Britons, Alfred the Great, Anglo-Saxons, Saxons, King Canute (King of Denmark, then England).
- Themes - raiding, invading other countries in Drakkars (Viking long-boats), Viking trade with other countries, territorial battles with Alfred the Great, Alfred's burning of the cakes, King Canute failing to hold back the incoming tide.
- 'Pieces' represent silver and gold, money, Danegeld (ransom money paid to stop invasions), materials to build Drakkars, villages taken over by the Vikings, Alfred's cakes.

Castle Game (Cordon Breaking)

Equipment: 'Pieces', a container, rope or sisal, stakes (in the absence of trees or other suitable upright).
Players: Any number.

• Set up a 'castle' with multiple entrances by roping off an area using stakes or trees. Ideally, the site should be surrounded by trees, scrub or other suitable hiding places. However ensure that there are more entrances than the number of guards, e.g. seven entrances and five guards, so guards need to organise themselves accordingly. Place the container in the centre of the 'castle'.
• Either divide the players into two teams or play as individuals taking on the role of 'attackers' and 'guards'.
• The attackers should make a base some distance from the castle out of sight of the guards where they should be issued 'pieces'. The aim of this game is for the attackers to get as many 'pieces' into the castle in the time allocated or for the guards to intercept the pieces.
• Attackers can only enter the castle through the proper entrances and once inside the castle they can not be caught by the guards, whereby they can safely deposit their 'piece' into the container located there.
• Guards attempt to protect the castle by trying to catch (tag) attackers before they enter the castle. However guards are not allowed within the castle compound (i.e. within the roped-off area). Every attacker caught must then hand over their piece immediately before they can then be released.
• If attackers are caught (tagged) by a guard they must hand over their 'piece' and return to their own base for a replacement.
• Guards should use some form of code e.g. points of the compass or numbers on a clock face as a means of warning each other from which direction attackers are approaching.

- The team or individual (attackers or defenders) that smuggles or captures the most 'pieces' is the winner.
- An option could be for individual attackers or attacking Patrols to compete against each other if they are issued with their own identifiable 'pieces' (i.e. coloured, numbered or signed) which can be counted at the end of the game.

Robin Hood (example)

- Maid Marion is being held prisoner within the walls of Nottingham castle. Robin's men equal the attacking team and the Sheriff's men the defending team.
- To rescue Marion, attackers need to get items of equipment (staves, sisal, etc.) past the castle guards and use them to construct a baluster (short pillar) in the centre of the castle.
- The baluster must fire a projectile (e.g. a tennis ball) the distance of the castle wall (sisal boundary) to allow her to escape.

Escape from Planet Zogg (example)

- It is the year 2040, and a group of spacemen have crash landed on the Planet Zogg. Their craft can still be flown but it has been stolen by the unfriendly Zoggites - natives of the planet, who are guarding it in a safe compound. The spacemen represent the attacking team, the Zoggites are the defenders.
- To escape the spacemen need to fill the craft's fuel tank with a litre of superfuel, which occurs naturally on the planet, and to get all members of the craft's crew inside the rocket compound, ready to escape.
- Superfuel is really water and the fuel tank is a container in the centre of the compound.

Global Warming battle (example)

• Our planet - Earth has a hole in its ozone layer allowing dangerous UV rays from the sun to pass through.
• To prevent the planet from warming up it is necessary to stop pollution, thus allowing the ozone layer to be rebuilt and provide better protection from the sun's rays.
• In this game attackers represent pollution, with UV rays the 'pieces' carried by the attacking team. Defenders are the ozone layer - a number of defenders located outside the boundary, and pollution stoppers, other members of the defending team located inside the boundary (i.e. on Earth). Earth is the 'castle' and the sun is the attackers base where 'pieces' are issued.
• The game starts with a depleted ozone layer (i.e. a minimal number of defenders positioned outside the boundary). Other defenders must attempt to stop 'pollution's' encroachment on Earth (inside the boundary) by undertaking a series of anti-pollution tasks.
• An example task could be to volley a ball (a pollutant molecule) to each member of the team without letting it touch the ground and dropping it into a bag (pollutant trap). This could be repeated until ten molecules have been trapped.
• For each task completed the ozone layer will be replenished (a defender from inside the boundary joins the defence on the outside). Each player added to the ozone layer reduces the warming by one degree. Every five players that get through the ozone layer and onto the planet increase warming by one degree.
• Who will win the battle of global warming?

Deforestation (example)

- Indigenous Brazilian Indian tribes are trying to protect 'their' rain forest from destruction. It is necessary for them therefore to persuade the authorities to cancel the permits held by foresters, who in the process of logging, are destroying the Indians' home.
- For the tribes to succeed they must get their message heard by Western countries. In this game the 'castle' is represented by the forest, the attacking team the foresters, the defending team are the indigenous Indians. A permit is the 'piece', each permit allows 10,000 trees to be destroyed. A permit can only be cancelled by a defender tagging an attacker.
- How many trees will be saved or destroyed?

Sun Protector (example)

- The effect of UV rays from direct sunlight on our skin can cause skin cancer, which is increasing drastically.
- Skin cancer can be avoided by stopping excessive sunlight from reaching people's skin. You can protect your body from the sun with clothing and by using sun protection of the right factor.
- For the purpose of this game, the 'castle' is represented by the skin, the attacking team are the UV rays, the defending team are sun protection and '100 deaths' is equal to one 'piece'.
- How many deaths can be prevented? Do Troop members know what factor cream is suitable for their own skin?
- An option could be to get defenders to carry cards showing the limit of their protection (e.g. factor eight). Each 'piece' carried by attackers also carries a factor number. If an attacker is caught by a defender with an equal or greater number then the defender wins the 'piece', otherwise the attacker is free to continue.

Running Rummy (man-hunt)

Equipment: A Pack of playing cards.
Players: Any number.

• Each Patrol forms a team and is dealt seven cards.
• Each Patrol must aim to collect two 'runs'- a run of three and a run of four.
A 'run' is either a set of cards which all carry the same face value or cards of the same suit in numerical order e.g. nine, ten, jack and the queen of diamonds.
• Cards can be exchanged through the game leader who is the 'dealer' for a different one. Dealer's make it difficult for players to find them by frequently changing hiding positions.
• Players can leave their base in pairs to find the dealer(s). Each pair may carry only one card.
• Players must hand the card to the dealer and pick a replacement. The dealer's cards should be shown to players face-down. Note: You can not re-exchange the card until you have returned to base with it first.
• The first team to show a hand of two rummy 'runs' to the game leader is the winner.
• An option could be that different dealers have specific cards e.g. black cards/red dealer, or a dealer for each suit.
• Dealers identify their location from time to time by blowing a whistle.

Delivery (cordon breaking)

Equipment: 'Pieces'.
Players: Any number.

• First set up two bases, A and B, with a leader at each. Identify the locations to each team by description or grid reference.

- Assign about a quarter of the available players, or one particular Patrol to be 'catchers' and the remainder to be 'carriers'.
- The carriers go to base A and collect a 'piece' where they must proceed to base B and hand over their 'piece' to the base leader then return to base A for another 'piece'.
- Points (or a reward item of some description) are awarded for each successfully delivered 'piece'.
- The catchers try to collect as many 'pieces' as possible by tagging carriers, but catchers are not allowed within 200 metres of either base.
- The winner can either be the individual or team that collects the most points (or rewards).

Heavy water (example)

- A Patrol represents the secret service of a major power with the aim of delivering as much 'heavy water' to a reactor as possible to produce 'pellets' of uranium.
- One cup of heavy water is needed to make one pellet and a scientist at the reactor will measure the quantity of water delivered, rewarding players with the appropriate number of pellets.
- International inspectors may be encountered en-route and will demand two cups of the water for inspection purposes.
- In this game 'heavy water' is tap water transported between bases in a container e.g. a billy. The source of the heavy water is base A, manned by the 'heavy water' manufacturer.
- Base B is the nuclear reactor, manned by a reactor scientist, the entrance to which is a challenging obstacle (a rope bridge or ladder) enhancing the chances for last minute spillage!
- The international inspectors are the catchers, whilst uranium pellets can be pieces of foil.

Variations on heavy water

• Return delivery - additional points are awarded if you return the reward back to base A.
• Multi-level delivery, where higher level bases are added, i.e. if players take the reward from base B to base C they receive an even higher reward. This in turn can be taken onto base D, etc. When a player is eventually tagged they must surrender all rewards collected to date except for the highest reward, then restart the game at the lowest level. The player(s) and team(s) with the highest amount of rewards wins the game.
• Chain delivery - a Patrol container is located at a number of sequential bases. For each 'piece' delivered from A to B the base leader will award two higher level 'pieces' and place them in your Patrol container. The same applies for delivery from B to C, and so on. To win your Patrol must get the greatest number of 'pieces' to the highest level container. The different level 'pieces' are visually different to prevent delivery directly from A to the highest base! You may only carry one 'piece' at a time. The game requires the Patrol Leader to use management skills to deploy the Patrol to cover the weak links in the supply chain.

Oregon Trail (man-hunt)

Equipment: 'Gold ingots' (e.g. gold coloured 'pieces' or barley sugars), 'silver ingots' (e.g. silver coloured 'pieces' or sugar lumps), 'bullion carrier' (e.g. a mug) per group containing two gold ingots.
Players: Any number.

• Divide the playing area into two halves - 'Goldland' and 'Silverland' with a defined strip of land representing a border crossing.

- Players should be divided into Patrols. (Patrols may be further divided into two or more groups depending on the amount of 'bullion' available).
- The aim is for teams to increase their holding of gold by as much as possible in the time allowed.
- In Goldland gold is more valuable than silver. Somewhere in the land you will find a bullion dealer (game leader) who is willing to exchange any ingots of gold for two ingots of silver (i.e. silver coloured 'pieces' or sugar lumps). Across the border in Silverland silver is more valuable than gold. You will find a dealer who will exchange any silver ingots for two gold ingots. Therefore teams will have to criss cross the border to undertake exchange deals.
- All the bullion must be carried in the team's bullion carriers at all times.
- The Patrol who collects the most gold ingots in the time allowed is the winner.
- An option could be for bullion thieves to operate in the vicinity of the border between Goldland and Silverland (but not around the dealers). If any member of a group is tagged by a thief they must forfeit half of their gold ingots. If a player is down to their last ingot this does not have to be forfeited.
- For a variation divide the players into two teams. One team represents Silverland and aims to collect silver, they can start off with two silver ingots. The other team represents Goldland and aims to collect Gold, starting with two Gold ingots.
- Bullion thieves operating near the border crossing, similarly, either represent Goldland or Silverland and will only take ingots from members of the opposing team.
- At the end of the game the side possessing the most ingots of the appropriate type, wins.

Interceptor

Equipment: Identical sets of cards, each set comprising of six cards numbered one to six (or labelled with various items according to a chosen storyline). You will need enough cards to make up approximately three sets per player.
Players: Any number.

• Choose six players to act as card 'carriers' - this role is ideal for Leaders and Helpers. The carriers' hold cards of only one type.
• The other players split into two teams - card 'collectors' and card 'interceptors'. Note: Carriers and collectors must agree on a password which is not known to the interceptors, for identification purposes.
• Collectors must try to collect a complete set of cards, one from each of the carriers, who they must find as they are allowed to hide (change hiding places as the game progresses).
• Collectors can assist each other by passing on the latest information about the location of the carriers. Players must be sure not to assist the interceptors by revealing the password!
• Collectors can not revisit a carrier for a replacement card until they have collected all the other cards in the set.
• Interceptors also try to collect sets of cards. They obtain a card by intercepting (tagging) a collector.
• If a collector is tagged by an interceptor they must show all their cards face down. The interceptor can then choose one and take it.
• Cards may be swapped between players of each team before but not after the game ends.
• The team (or individual, if you choose) that collects the most sets of cards is the winner.

Escape from Urkon (example)

• Location is the planet Urkon.
• Characters - collectors represent spacemen from Earth who have crashed on the planet Urkon. Interceptors represent war-making aliens who have invaded Urkon and wish to obtain the same items as the spacemen which will enable them to invade more planets. Carriers are native Urkonites, who are peace loving, harmless creatures, very shy and difficult to find. The Urkonites wish to help the Earthmen but not the interceptors and, therefore, require evidence of the Earthmen's identity by way of a password before handing over their items.
• 'Pieces' are items that are required to help in the escape from the planet (e.g. a spaceship, fuel, food, oxygen, supply cards labelled appropriately).

Laser Vision (man hunt)

Equipment: Paper, pens, safety pins.
Players: Any number.

• Attach an individual three figure number, written on a piece of paper, to the back and front of each player with safety pins.
• Each player attempts to track the other players to get their numbers which they have written down on a list.
• Each player must ensure that other players do not get to see their number by 'hiding' at appropriate moments.
Note: players can not cover up their numbers unfairly e.g. by covering it with clothing.
• For each number recorded players score a hit. Scores will be calculated by the game leader by taking the number of successful hits and subtracting the number of times players were hit by others.
• The player with the highest score is the winner. For the players' interest produce a table showing who hit who.

Play Your Cards Right (man-hunt)

Equipment: One or ideally two or more packs of playing cards. Alternatively prepare numbered cards, a different colour for each Patrol.
Players: Any number.

• Divide the players either into Patrols or into two teams and allocate the name of a playing card suit (diamonds, hearts, etc.) to each Patrol or allocate a colour (red or black) if there are only two teams.
• Have two leaders - A, who carries the cards and B, who carries a 'post box'. Both leaders must hide in separate locations which they frequently change.
• Each card is worth the same in points as its face value - one point for an ace up to ten points for a picture card. Aces have no special power above other cards in this game. Although picture cards carry the same points; a King defeats a Queen, which defeats Jack. Cards won in challenges will give teams valuable bonus points. Keep them until the end of the game. Do not 'post' them.
• Players search out leader A whereupon players state their Patrol's suit, resulting in Patrol's being issued with a single card of that suit randomly. Players then search out the post box carried by leader B and post it, returning to leader A for another card.
• At any point in the game Patrols may challenge each other by tagging members of the other team. When tagged carriers and challengers alike, must reveal their cards at the same time. The Patrol with the highest card keeps both cards. If the cards are equal both groups retain their original card.
• The team with the largest number of 'posted' points plus bonus points is the winner.

Silent Approach (man-hunt)

Equipment: An armband or bandanna per player of a distinctive colour for each Patrol.
Players: Any number.

• Each Patrol goes to a different location but of an equal walking distance from a proposed meeting point. Teams must be provided with maps, compasses and the grid references of the drop off point and meeting point.
• The objective is, whilst walking to the meeting point, for Patrols to spot other participating Patrols first.
• When one Patrol has spotted two others and can name the colour they are wearing then that Patrol reveals themselves to the game leader.
• The Patrol giving the correct information first to the game leader is the winner.

King Arthur and his silent knights

• Location - Camelot. King Arthur has summoned his knights to a meeting at Camelot. Arthur, weary of intrusion by the evil Black Knight, has asked each knight and his entourage to wear armbands of the same colour. This colour is only known to a true knight of the Round Table.
• Characters - players are servants employed by the knights to support them on their journey and to 'scout' the area in advance checking for the parties of other knights. By spotting the colour worn by the other knights' party players will be able to deduce the identity of the Black Knight. It is important for 'scouts' to remain well hidden (players must not remove or cover up their armbands). When the identity of the Black Knight is known (the Patrol Leader or the Patrol wearing the wrong coloured armbands), warn Arthur, who is located in the vicinity of Camelot. As a reward the winning Patrol will be made knights too!

Four-two-one (man-hunt)

Equipment: Cards numbered one, two or four.
Players: Eight or more.

• First off, issue a single card to each player bearing either number one, two or four.
• Those players holding the 'four' card join together in groups of four and aim to tag players with card 'two'. Likewise, players with the 'two' card join together in pairs and aim to tag players with card 'one'. Players holding card 'one' go around individually and try to tag players with card 'four'.
• If a player(s) successfully catches a group that they are chasing (i.e. tag any player from the group), then the tagged group must distribute their cards evenly amongst the chasers and then return to base for replacements.
• Replacement cards are issued randomly by the game leader so players may be issued with a new number. Note, players must remain at the base until there are enough players with the same number to form a team.
• At the end of the game add up the number of complete sets of cards (a set equals four 'fours', two 'twos' or one 'one') acquired by your team.
• The team with the most complete sets is the winner.

Forty-Forty (man-hunt)

Equipment: None.
Players: Any number.

• First, nominate a player the 'seeker' and choose a base such as a tree stump in a clearing surrounded by trees or scrub.
• All the players should go and hide with the exception of the seeker who remains at base.

- Players aim to get to the base without being spotted by the seeker.
- If a seeker shouts 'forty-forty' (plus player's name) and points in the player's direction, they must give themselves up and drop out of the game. Remember this game relies on honesty.
- When the opportunity arises (i.e. when the seeker is away from the base looking for players) players can run and touch the base and shout 'forty-forty home'.
- If a player achieves this before the seeker can touch the base then they have successfully made it home. The first player home scores 10 points for their Patrol, the second nine points and so on.
- The team with the highest number of points after players have made it home or are 'out' is the winner.

Kick The Dead Donkey

Equipment: Any object.
Players: Any number.

- First nominate a player as the seeker.
- Rather than using a base, place an object (the 'dead donkey') in the centre of the clearing.
- Any player who successfully reaches and 'kicks' the object without getting tagged or named by the seeker scores points as above.
- The seeker must point in the exact right direction when naming a player who, when named, must give themselves up.
- The player with the most points is the winner.

RAIDS

There are essentially two types of base raid games - with many variations! In the first type the aim is to collect as many 'lives' from opponents' as possible whilst protecting one's own. The second type of raid game may also involve 'lives' but the principle aim is to get one or more items from an opponent's base(s) to one's own base. This section describes both types of game and suggests a number of variations.

Designing your own raid game
To design your own raid game give consideration to the following key elements:
• Team bases - where they are located, how to get in, what they represent, how they are defended.
• 'lives' - what to use, the way in which it can be lost to opponents and how a player can get a new one. (Games in which players must challenge each other for possession of a 'life' offer plenty of scope for variation.)
• Items to be raided - how they are obtained, how they are transported and what they represent.

Tips for successful raid games
• Items to be raided should not be unfairly hidden.
• Bases should be roughly the same distance apart and the distance between bases should be appropriate to the intended playing time and to the difficulty of the task.
• Guards should not defend so closely or in such numbers that the task is too difficult. It may help to define an exclusion zone that prevents 'guards' from getting too close to items they are defending. Castle raids are usually quite successful for this reason.

Simple Base Raid

Equipment: A container of 'pieces' for each Patrol.
Players: As Patrols.

- First, players should form into Patrol teams.
- Patrol's choose a base known only to them, and position their container of 'pieces' on the ground. The container must be positioned in an open space visible from at least three paces away in any direction.
- The aim of the game is for players to bring back as many 'pieces' as possible from an opponents base whilst at the same time protecting their own 'pieces'.
- Players must take only one 'piece' from a base on each visit.
- Patrols keep the location of their base a secret by hiding. If players hide too close to their own base it could help opponents locate it.
- If there is a danger from opponent's locating a team's base, attempts can be made to remove the opponent's 'life' thus forcing them to return to base for a new one.
- Half the Patrol should guard the base and the other half should go in search of opponents' bases. If a player loses a 'life' they must return to a central base for a new one.
- The team that makes the greatest net profit in 'pieces' i.e. 'pieces' gained less 'pieces' lost, is the winner.
- A scoring system could be devised that also takes into account 'lives' gained and lost.

Classic Trophy Raid

Equipment: A single 'trophy' per base (a trophy is essentially any object that can be easily carried), 'lives'.
Players: Any number.

• Follow the principles for the simple base raid game above, but apply the following modifications.
• The game ends as soon as a team successfully gets another team's trophy back to their own base.
• If a player who is carrying another team's trophy is tagged, then the trophy belongs to the tagger and the same player can not retake it. If a player tags a player who is carrying their own Patrol's trophy, the trophy is immediately safe and can not be retaken on its way back to their base.
• Patrol flags were once the usual 'trophy' in raid games and the name 'flag raid' is still commonly used to describe this type of game. In the days when wide games were commonly played across very large areas the capturing of a single trophy was no easy task. You may find that playing this game in a relatively confined area that the game finishes a little too quickly. For a solution to this see Perpetual Trophy Raid.

Perpetual Trophy Raid

Equipment: Two trophies per team, 'lives'.
Players: Any number.

• Follow the principles for the simple base raid game above, but with the following modifications.
• The aim is for each team to get four trophies in total back to their base, or to hold the greatest number of trophies when the game ends.
• Teams can only raid one trophy from a base at a time and trophies must be raided from at least two different bases.

Castle Raid

Equipment: A container of 'pieces' or a number of trophies, rope and stakes to make the castle, 'lives'.
Players: Any number.

• This is simply a version of the castle game in which the aim is to raid 'pieces' or 'trophies' from the castle rather than smuggling items into it.
• The only addition is that attackers must carry 'lives'.
• Play it with a single castle and a dedicated set of guards.
• The team that succeeds in the quickest time is the winner.

Multi-castle Raid

Equipment: For each patrol - two trophies or a container of 'pieces', rope and staves with which to construct a castle, 'lives'.
Players: Any number.

• Each Patrol team sets up their own castle with four entrances.
• Three members of each team must stay to guard the castle, the other players attempt to raid the other castles.
• Teams are not allowed inside their own castle.
• The game can be based on raiding 'pieces' or 'trophies' and scoring should be based on the amount of trophies and lives won or lost.

Get A Life!

Equipment: A 'life' for each player and three spare 'lives' per Patrol left at the Patrol base. (No extra 'lives' are issued during the game.)
Players: Any number.

- Get each player to number off in their Patrols. Players must write their individual number on the top of their hand.
- Each Patrol is allocated a base, similar in distances from each other. Note: the bases of other Patrols are strictly out of bounds.
- If a player obtains the 'life' of an opponent from another team - which can be won or lost by tagging, they take it immediately to their base. Players must not keep hold of 'lives' as another Patrol member could be waiting to challenge them for it.
- Once challenged, opponents must show their number to each other. Players who have a lower number must surrender their 'life' and vice versa.
- The exception is that a player numbered 'one' defeats any number greater than four. If the numbers are equal then neither player loses a 'life'.
- If a player loses a 'life' they must return to their base for a new one. If a 'life' is not available a player will have to wait until a member of their Patrol brings one in.
- To win the players will need to work as a team. (A suggested team strategy could be to send out the safest numbers early on in the game to learn the numbers of the other players, reporting back so that the whole of the Patrol can then compete more effectively.
- The team that makes the greatest net gain of 'lives' in the time allowed is the winner.

Lighthouse (treasure hunt)

Equipment: A flashing light, (Alternatively use a distinctive torch, siren or radio.) torches.
Players: Any number.

• Assemble players at one end of the playing area selected for the game. Place the light etc., towards the end furthest away.
• Get Leaders or older Scouts to patrol the area with torches looking for any sign of movement.
• If any part of a player is caught moving in the torches beam they must return immediately to the starting line.
• The aim of this game is for players to attempt to be the first to locate a flashing light that has been hidden in the area in front of them and turn it on.
• To avoid being caught in the 'guards' light it is recommended that players stalk their way slowly, keeping as low as possible, until they reach the flashing light.
• The first player to locate the light and turn it on is the winner. (This is a simple night time game suitable for playing in a field or in open woodland.)

TRAINING GAMES

Games that can be used as exercises to teach or test specific Scout skills.

The Scout Law Game

Equipment: Give each team a copy of the same edition of a newspaper(s).
Players: Any number.

• Divide all the players into teams and give each one a copy of a newspaper - the same edition.
• The teams should read through the newspaper(s) and cut out pictures and stories that illustrate some aspect of the Scout Law. (This could also apply to values and the Promise.)
• For example, number the cuttings to correspond with the appropriate aspect of the Law - remember there are seven in total. The team which collects the largest number of clippings in the given time is the winner.

Headline Race

Equipment: Identical newspapers for each team.
Players: Any number.

• First, divide all the players into teams and allocate each team the same edition of a newspaper.
• The game leader will read out brief details of a story from the same edition of the paper that each team has.
• The first team to find the story in their edition and shout out the headline to the story will score a point.
• The team which scores the most points is the winner.

Map Bingo

Equipment: For each team - identical maps, bingo cards showing mapping symbols.
Players: Any number.

• First, divide all the players into appropriate sized teams.
• The game leader - the 'caller' should shout out some six-figure grid references which highlight regular OS map symbols.
• Each team has 30 seconds to find it on their map and cross it off if it corresponds with a symbol on their 'bingo' card.
• The first team to complete its card and shout out *'Ordnance Survey!'* is the winner.

North, South, East And West

Equipment: None required.
Players: Any number.

• Name four sides of the playing area North, South, East and West. The corners correspond with the intermediate compass directions. North-East, South-East, South-West and North-West.
• When the game leader calls out a direction, say *'North-West'*, all the players must run to the appropriate allocated wall or corner.
• Players will be out if the game leader judges them to be too slow or are seen heading in the wrong direction.
• The last Scout remaining 'in' is the winner.
• The game could be made more complicated by allocating a new wall or even a corner as North with the other walls changing relative to this.

Traditional Kim's Game

Equipment: A large assortment of small articles and objects, a tray and something to cover the objects with.
Players: Any number.

• Put the items on a tray or table out of view until the game starts.
• Each player has two minutes to study all the items put on view.
• The game leader should then cover or remove the items.
• Each player has to report back each item remembered.
• Award a point for each item remembered. (It is normal to ask for items to be written down, but the report back could be verbal.)
• The winner is the one who scores the most points for remembering the most items.

Missing Kim's

Equipment: A large assortment of small articles and objects, a tray, something to cover the objects with.
Players: Any number.

• The players have two minutes to study the items on display.
• The game leader should then remove one or more of the items.
• The players must then aim to identify correctly the missing items.
• Players score a point for each missing object correctly identified.
• Alternatively substitute objects with well-known smells or sounds, or read out (twice over) a list of objects beginning with the same letter, for players to remember.

Whose Hand?

Equipment: Something to cover or partially hide behind.
Players: Any number.

• Divide all the players into Patrol teams.
• Each Patrol should study the hands of all the other Scouts playing the game.
• One Patrol should then go out of view, where one member of which, should reveal only their hands e.g. from behind a curtain or something similar, to the rest of the players.
• The other players (not of the hidden Patrol) then have the task of guessing who the owner of the hands is?
• The first Patrol to name the Patrol whose member is showing off their hands is the winner.

Description

Equipment: Any object with distinguishable features.
Players: Any number.

• Hold up for example, a pencil and ask players what they can see? Hopefully the response will be a pencil!
• Now ask what can be observed? The response should highlight its grade, the manufacturer, its sharpness, colour, possibly a few nicks, etc.
• This game will highlight the fact that many people see but not many observe, which is a useful skill to develop.
• Award points for the most observations.
• The team with the most points is the winner.

Observation

Equipment: Any object.
Players: Any number.

• Players will be given an object and are allowed to study it for one minute.
• The game leader should then remove the object.
• The objective of this game is for players or teams to describe as many features of the object as possible.
• The person (or Patrol) who gives the most detailed description is the winner.

Rising Circles

Equipment: None.
Players: 10 - 12 players.

• Divide the players into teams of around five or six and get each team to form a circle.
• All the players of each team sit down cross-legged with their hands placed on the other team members' shoulders.
• The aim of the game is for each team to try to stand up together without letting go of each other.
• The first team to stand up is the winner.

Race The Ball

Equipment: One football.
Players: Any number.

• Get all the players to form a circle and allocate one player to be on the outside.
• Players should then pass the football clockwise around the circle twice.
• During this time the player on the outside tries to run around the circle as many times as possible.
• The game should be repeated with different players as runners.
• The runner who achieves the greatest number of circuits in a given time is the winner.

GAMES KEY

To help you with a quick reference guide, each game indexed, is followed by a series of coded entries as referred to in the key guide below. It should make choosing the right game for the right occasion much easier. The first entry will apply to equipment, the second to the number of players and the final entry refers to venue preparation.

Equipment

No	nothing special required to play
⚽	a football/ball is required
⚽ ⚽ ⚽	the number of balls required
Yes	the game requires some special equipment

Numbers

Any	any number can play
6+	at least six players needed
12+(2T)	at least 12 are needed to play in two teams
2P+	two teams or Patrols or more

Venue Preparation

No	can be played in any large room, hall or play area, but it is assumed you can define areas and lines
Yes	you will need to set up the game area before playing
Optional	game area can be set up specifically, but this is not essential to the game

INDEX

A
Activity Races	Yes	Any	No	47
All Out Rule				74
Ankle Push	No	6+(2T)	No	24

B
Back of the Queue	Yes	2P+	No	56
Backwards Punchball	⚽	10+	No	13
Balloon Blow	Yes	2P+	No	41
Banana Race	Yes	Any	No	48
Barge	No	Any	No	22
Big Kick	⚽	8+(2T)	No	76
Box Ball	⚽	8+(2T)	Yes	69
Bull's-eye	No	6+(2T)	Yes	21

C
Cambridge Boat Race	No	10+	No	27
Camel Races	Yes	2P+	Yes	51
Camel Races (Options)	Yes	2P+	Yes	51
Castle Game	Yes	Any	Yes	91
Castle Raid	Yes	Any	Yes	108
Casualty	⚽	Any	Yes	10
Circle Relay	Yes	2P+	No	55
Classic Relay	Yes	2P+	No	54
Classic Trophy Raid	Yes	Any	Yes	107
Confined Kingball	⚽	Any	No	11
Continuous Cricket	Yes	8+(2T)	Yes	77
Continuous Punchball	⚽	10+	No	12
Cowboys and Indians	No	8+(2T)	No	36
Crazy Rounders	Yes	8+(2T)	Yes	81
Crowded Circle	No	Any	No	13

D

Defend the Garrison	⚽	8+(2T)	Yes	35
Deforestation	Yes	Any	Yes	94
Delivery	Yes	Any	Yes	95
Description	Yes	Any	Yes	114
Diagonal relay	Yes	2P+	Yes	54
Dividing Amoebae	No	8+	No	15
Dizzy	Yes	Any	No	48
Dodger	⚽	Any	No	8
Dog and Bone	Yes	6+(2T)	No	20
Double Football	⚽	8+(2T)	Yes	73
Down the Line	Yes	2P+	No	56
Dragstore	Yes	12+(3T+)	Yes	45
Drop Ball	Yes	12+(2T)	No	75
Duel	Yes	6+(2T)	No	19

E

Elephant Relay	No	2P+	No	58
Environmental	Yes	Any	Yes	89
Escape from the planet Zogg	Yes	Any	Yes	92
Escape from Urkon	Yes	Any	Yes	100

F

Four-Two-One	Yes	8+	No	103
Forty-Forty	No	Any	No	103
Flying Disc Base	Yes	8+	Yes	80
Flying Disc Golf	Yes	4+(2T)	Yes	72

G

Game for a laugh	No	6+(2T)	No	39
Games Key				117
Get a Life!	No	Any	No	109
Global Warming Battle	Yes	Any	Yes	93
Goal Catcher	⚽	8+(2T)	Yes	69
Grab	Yes	6+	Yes	15
Great Divide, The	No	6+(2T)	No	37
Guardian of the Jewel	No	8+	No	33

H

Hare and Hound	No	10+	No	26
Head It! Catch It!	☺	Any	No	17
Headline Race	Yes	Any	Yes	111
Heavy Water	Yes	Any	Yes	96
Heavy Water (variation)	Yes	Any	Yes	97
Human Bowls	☺	6+(2T)	No	47
Human Clock Relay	☺	10+(2T)	No	61
Human Noughts and Crosses	Yes	6+	No	33

I

In and out of the Houses	No	8+	No	29
Indoor Rounders	Yes	8+(2T)	Yes	83
Interceptor	Yes	Any	Yes	99

J

Jockey	No	8+	No	26

K

Kangaroo Hop	☺☺☺	Any	Opt	49
Kick the Dead Donkey	Yes	Any	Yes	104
King Arthur and his Silent Knights	Yes	Any	Yes	102
King Arthur and the Round Table	Yes	Any	Yes	90
Kingball	☺	Any	No	11
Knock Off Ground Tag	Yes	Any	Yes	9
Knock-out	☺	6+	Yes	66

L

Laser Vision	Yes	Any	Yes	100
Lead Football	Yes	6+(2T)	Yes	35
Lighthouse	Yes	Any	No	110
Link-ball	☺	8+	No	14
'Lives'				86
Long Goal	☺	12+(2T)	No	65

M

Map Bingo	Yes	Any	No	112
Matchbox	Yes	6+(2T)	No	22
Message Relay	Yes	2P+	No	59
Missing Kim's	Yes	Any	Yes	113
Multi-castle Raid	Yes	Any	Yes	108
Multi-team Football	⚽⚽⚽	9+(3T)	Yes	67
Multi-team Tug of War	Yes	12+(3T+)	No	42

N

No Bowler Cricket	Yes	6+(2T)	Yes	76
North, South, East and West	No	Any	No	112

O

Observation	Yes	Any	No	115
Off Ground Tag	Yes	Any	Yes	8
One-Two-Three-Four	No	Any	No	49
Oregon Trail	Yes	Any	Yes	97
Over and Under	⚽	2P+	No	58
Overtake	⚽⚽	8+(2T)	No	38

P

Pair Swap	No	8+	N0	28
Pair's Hockey	Yes	6+(2T)	No	19
Pair's Long Goal	⚽	12+	No	29
Pass the Object	Yes	2P+	Yes	57
Pea and Paper	Yes	Any	No	48
Penguin Ball	No	6+(2T)	No	68
Perpetual Trophy Raid	Yes	Any	Yes	107
Pick It Up	No	12+	No	9
'Pieces'				85
Pillow Fight	Yes	6+(2T)	Yes	24
Play your Cards Right	Yes	Any	Yes	101
Point of no Return	Yes	Any	No	20
Poison	Yes	Any	No	14
Poke and Push	Yes	6+(2T)	No	24
Punchball	⚽	10+	No	12

Q
Quiz Swap	No	Any	No	30

R
Race the Ball	⚽	Any	No	116
Ring of Steel	⚽	8+(2T)	Yes	38
Rising Circles	No	10+	No	115
Robin and Little John	No	6+(2T)	Yes	21
Robin Hood	Yes	Any	Yes	88, 92
Roll Ball	⚽⚽⚽⚽	8+(2T)	No	66
Rucsac Relay	Yes	2P+	No	60
Run the Risk	⚽⚽⚽⚽	8+(2T)	No	32
Runaround Quiz	Yes	Any	Yes	16
Running Rummy	Yes	Any	Yes	95

S
Scout Law Game, The	Yes	Any	Yes	111
Shuttle Relay	Yes	2P+	No	55
Sicilian Shove	No	6+(2T)	Yes	46
Silent Approach	Yes	Any	Yes	102
Simple Base Raid	Yes	2P+	Yes	106
Six	Yes	8+	No	10
Snatch and Grab	No	8+	No	23
Spoon Feeding	Yes	2P+	No	57
Star Trek	Yes	Any	Yes	89
Stave Tug	Yes	Any	No	23
Staves	Yes	2P+	No	59
Storm the Castle	No	12+(3T)	No	41
Submarines	Yes	8+(2T)	No	34
Sun Protector	Yes	Any	Yes	94

T
Target Ball	⚽	6+(2T)	Yes	66
Target Ball (variation)	⚽	6+(2T)	Yes	67
Team Pass Football	⚽	6+(2T)	Yes	72
The Great Divide	No	6+(2T)	No	37
Theatre Race	Yes	Any	No	49
Throw Home	Yes	6+(2T)	Yes	78

Thrower-Catcher	⊙ ⊙ ⊙ ⊙	8+(2T)	No	32
Tip and Run	No	6+	No	28
Tom and Jerry	No	12+	No	30
Touch Rugby	⊙	8+(2T)	No	70
Trader	Yes	Any	No	7
Trading Post	Yes	8+(2T)	Yes	42
Trading Post (Options)	Yes	8+(2T)	Yes	44
Traditional Kim's Game	Yes	Any	Any	113
Training Miscellany	Yes	6+(2T)	No	25
Training Races	Yes	6+(2T)	No	50
Transfer Relay	Yes	2P+	No	63
Triangular Rounders	⊙	8+(2T)	Yes	80
Tripod Football	⊙ Yes	4+(2T)	No	71
Trust your Guide	Yes	2P+	Yes	62

V

Vikings and Alfred the Great, The	Yes	Any	Yes	90

W

Water!	Yes	2P+	Yes	57
Weavers Relay	No	2P+	No	63
Whirling Wheel	⊙	2P+	No	61
Whose Hand?	Yes	Any	Yes	114

Z

Zone Ball	⊙	8+(2T)	Yes	31